FOREVER AND EVER

The Art of Partnership and Building a Resilient Marriage

Homer Hargrove

Cover Design: Homer Hargrove

Published by: Homer Hargrove

For more information, visit: www.homerhargrove.com

ISBN: 9798339708667

Printed in the United States of America.

First Edition

Dedication

To Lauren Hargrove,

My beautiful wife, my best friend, and my greatest supporter. Our love is the foundation upon which this book is built. Your kindness and grace inspire me daily.

This book is as much yours as it is mine. Your insights, your patience, and your relentless belief in our mission have shaped every word and idea. Thank you for walking beside me, for lifting me up when I am weak, and for loving me with a love that is so pure and genuine.

This is for you, Lauren—my forever and ever soulmate. May we continue to grow together, and may our journey inspire others to find the same joy and fulfillment in their own marriages.

You will always have my heart.

About the Author: Homer Hargrove is a seasoned professional speaker and minister with over a decade of experience. He currently serves as the pastor of Gravetop Church and hosts the "Hidden Potential" podcast, where he inspires individuals to surpass their own expectations through practical leadership and personal growth strategies.

Homer's journey began with a life marred by trauma, addiction, and violence. His turning point came when he decided to reach beyond himself and embrace a higher purpose. Today, he passionately believes that every person holds untapped potential waiting to be unlocked.

Homer is dedicated to his family, as a loving husband to Lauren Hargrove and a devoted father to their three children: Joy Love, Jewels Mercy, and Homer IV. He has spent over ten years becoming a professional in speaking, leadership, and ministry. He now serves as the Senior Pastor of Gravetop Church, which he established in San Antonio, TX.

Throughout his career, Homer has developed and launched impactful ministries, leaving a positive mark in recovery centers, public schools, detention centers, and various other organizations. Known for his sense of humor and unwavering resolve, Homer delivers essential tools to empower and equip individuals, presenting his insights in a clear, articulate, and practical manner. Connect with him at homerhargrove.com.

Table Of Contents

Acknowledgements

First and foremost, I want to thank God for guiding us through this journey and for His unwavering presence in our lives and ministry. Without His grace and wisdom, this book would not have been possible.

To those of you who have supported and sowed into us and our ministry, your support has meant the world to us. For every prayer, word of encouragement, and act of love, we are forever grateful. You believed in us when we were just getting started, and your faith in the work we were doing kept us going in moments of uncertainty.

To those who have stood by us over the years, whether in the early days of ministry or through the challenges that followed, we cannot thank you enough. Your belief in our calling, your generosity, and your partnership have made a lasting impact not just on us, but on every life we've been able to reach together.

This book is a reflection of the love and support you've shown us, and we dedicate it to all of you who have walked this road with us. Your encouragement has strengthened our hearts and empowered us to continue the work that God has set before us.

Thank you for believing in us and for being a part of this incredible journey.

INTRODUCTION

Welcome to "Forever And Ever: The Art of Partnership and Building a Resilient Romantic Marriage." This book is designed to be a practical guide for couples who aspire to build a strong, enduring partnership grounded in love, trust, and mutual respect. Whether you're dating, engaged, or in a long-term commitment, these insights will help you strengthen your bond and navigate the journey of love with wisdom and grace.

In a world where relationships are constantly tested by life's challenges, it's more important than ever to equip ourselves with the tools needed to cultivate a resilient partnership. This book is born out of my years of experience in leadership, counseling, and ministry, where I've had the privilege of walking alongside countless couples at different stages of their journey toward a deeper, more fulfilling relationship.

Throughout the pages of this book, we'll explore the fundamental aspects that contribute to a thriving relationship—understanding and embracing differences, mastering the art of clear communication, fostering adaptability, nurturing intimacy and trust, and demonstrating unwavering commitment. These are not just abstract concepts but actionable principles that you can implement in your daily life, no matter the stage or nature of your relationship.

I believe every relationship has the potential to flourish, no matter the obstacles it faces. By embracing the journey of partnership and committing to continuous growth and understanding, you can create a bond that not only endures but also brings immense joy and fulfillment.

Whether you're just starting out as a couple or have been together for years, this book offers valuable insights and practical advice to help you navigate the complexities of your relationship. It's about building a foundation that can withstand the test of time, a relationship that is resilient, loving, and enduring.

As you embark on this journey, I encourage you to approach each chapter with an open heart and mind. Reflect on your relationship, discuss the insights with your partner, and embrace the principles with a willingness to grow together. Your relationship is a unique and beautiful journey, and I'm honored to be a part of it through this book.

Together, let's explore the art of partnership and build a resilient relationship that truly stands the test of time.

SECTION 1 - LEARNING HOW YOU BOTH LOVE & COMMUNICATE DIFFERENTLY

The goal of this section is to help you build a deeper understanding of each other. It's about recognizing that your partner may think and feel differently than you, and that's okay. You're not meant to force them to see things exactly the way you do; instead, learning to appreciate these differences can strengthen your bond.

We'll explore some common psychological differences that can arise in relationships, whether due to gender, upbringing, or personal experiences. We'll look at how these differences might impact your relationship and how understanding them can actually bring you closer together. Additionally, we'll dive into the unique ways each person processes emotions. Everyone handles their feelings in their own way, and recognizing these differences allows you to better support and connect with each other.

Another key focus is on communication and love. Every individual communicates and receives love differently. By understanding your partner's love language and communication style, you can deepen your connection and ensure that both of you feel seen, valued, and appreciated.

Ultimately, this section is about fostering empathy and appreciation for your partner's unique perspective. By embracing your differences, you'll not only create a more harmonious relationship but also a partnership grounded in mutual respect and love.

CHAPTER 1: THE DIFFERENCES IN PEOPLE

We all crave to feel loved, appreciated, and understood. These fundamental needs shape our lives and influence how we connect with others. But here's the thing: the ways we perceive and express these feelings can vary wildly from person to person.

Understanding and navigating these differences is crucial for building a healthy relationship. It means stepping out of your comfort zone and learning how your partner experiences love and appreciation. For Lauren and me, this journey involves active listening, empathy, and genuinely trying to see the world from each other's perspectives. By doing so, we bridge gaps that could lead to misunderstandings and unmet needs, fostering deeper and more meaningful connections.

Effective communication is the key to unlocking growth and harmony in any relationship. It's not just about clearly expressing our feelings and needs but also about being open to how our partner does the same. When both partners commit to understanding and respecting each other's differences, they create a dynamic and supportive environment. This strengthens the relationship, making it more fulfilling and resilient. Ultimately, learning to navigate these differences together enriches your partnership, making it more compassionate and harmonious.

WAFFLE AND SPAGHETTI MINDS

When it comes to how we think and process information in relationships, people tend to fall into two general categories: waffle minds and spaghetti minds. These are just fun analogies that help explain some of the differences in how we approach conversations, problem-solving, and even emotional processing. Understanding where you and your partner stand can help you communicate better and avoid unnecessary frustrations.

Let's start with the waffle mind. Picture a waffle with its neat grid of little compartments. People with a "waffle mind" tend to think of each thought, conversation, or experience as fitting into its own separate box. In relationships, this means they often focus on one thing at a time. For example, if they're discussing a problem, they prefer to solve that issue completely before moving on to anything else. It's like they want to make sure every box is dealt with before opening the next one. This methodical approach can be really effective for getting things done and solving problems, but it might come across as a little detached or overly segmented to someone who thinks differently. To their partner, it may seem like they're ignoring emotions or other factors if those don't fit neatly into the current "box" they're working on.

Now, think of a plate of spaghetti where everything is tangled together. People with "spaghetti minds" don't separate their thoughts and experiences into individual boxes. For them, everything is interconnected. One thought leads to another, and then another, in a continuous web of connections. In relationships, this often means that a spaghetti-minded person might talk about multiple topics in the same conversation, weaving together different thoughts, memories, and emotions as they go. They see the world in a more holistic way, where everything relates to everything else. This can lead to deeper insights and more emotionally rich conversations, but it can also feel overwhelming or scattered to someone who prefers a more compartmentalized approach, like the waffle mind.

If you're someone with a "waffle mind," you likely prefer clear and direct conversations where each issue is handled one at a time. It's all about focusing on one problem, resolving it fully, and then moving on to the next. This approach helps keep things organized and manageable. On the other hand, if you have more of a "spaghetti mind," your conversations probably flow in many directions. You might jump from one topic to another as different thoughts, feelings, and memories naturally connect. For you, everything is intertwined, so a single conversation might cover a range of topics that all seem linked in some way.

When it comes to conflict, waffle-minded individuals prefer to isolate the issue and work through it step by step. They're focused on breaking the conflict into manageable parts, solving one piece at a time. Too many issues brought up at once can feel overwhelming. Meanwhile, those with a spaghetti mind view conflict as multi-layered, where emotions, past experiences, and the present situation are all connected. They tend to address several related issues at once because, for them, it's hard to separate one part of the conflict from the bigger picture.

Emotionally, waffle minds process feelings in stages, sorting through them one at a time. Each emotion gets its own space to be addressed before moving on to the next. This methodical approach helps them manage their feelings in a structured way. In contrast, spaghetti minds experience emotions as a web of connections, with one feeling leading to another. They often feel and express a mix of emotions all at once, making it difficult to separate one specific feeling from the broader emotional landscape they're navigating.

QUANTITY AND QUALITY THINKING

In any relationship, how we think about and measure our experiences can make a big difference. Some of us are more focused on quantity, while others are all about quality. These two perspectives shape how we experience love, connection, and even how we handle day-to-day interactions.

If you're a quantity thinker, numbers matter to you. It's not just about what happens but how much it happens. Whether it's the number of activities you do together, the frequency of conversations, or the amount of time spent with your partner, quantity thinkers feel secure and loved when there's an abundance of something. For example, a quantity thinker might feel happiest when you're regularly going on dates, consistently exchanging gifts, or spending hours in conversation each day. The more frequent these interactions are, the stronger and more secure the connection feels to them.

Quality thinkers, on the other hand, focus less on how often something happens and more on the value behind it. For them, it's all about the meaning, depth, and emotional significance of each interaction. A quality thinker cherishes a meaningful conversation, even if it happens less frequently, because the emotional connection feels rich and deep. It's not about the number of gifts given, but the thought and care that went into choosing a particular gift. Quality thinkers care more about how special a moment feels rather than how often it happens. It's about the significance of the experience, not the frequency.

These two perspectives can sometimes cause tension if we don't recognize the differences in how we think. A quantity-focused person might feel like they're not getting enough attention because they crave frequent interactions. Meanwhile, a quality-focused person might feel like the connection is shallow if those interactions lack depth or meaning. By understanding which approach resonates more with you and your partner, you can begin to appreciate these differences and find ways to meet each other's needs.

If you're a quantity thinker, you're likely to emphasize regular check-ins. You might send frequent texts, make small gestures of love often, or just make sure you're communicating consistently. It's all about staying connected through regular, everyday interactions. On the flip side, if you're more of a quality thinker, you're probably looking for deeper conversations. It's not about how often you talk, but how meaningful those talks are. You value the richness of each interaction, making sure that every conversation has emotional depth and significance.

When it comes to resolving conflicts, quantity thinkers are usually focused on addressing issues as they come up. They want to resolve problems quickly and keep things running smoothly by tackling one issue after another. Quality thinkers, however, like to take their time. They want to dive deep into the root cause of the conflict, exploring all the emotions and reasons behind it. Their goal is to fully understand what's going on so they can find a resolution that really lasts, even if it takes a bit longer.

For quantity thinkers, feeling connected is all about frequency. They feel most loved when there are frequent interactions and regular demonstrations of affection. It's about knowing that you're present and engaged with them on a regular basis. Quality thinkers, however, feel connected through significant moments. It's not about how many interactions you have, but how deep and emotionally rich those interactions are. They feel closest to their partner when there's a strong emotional exchange during those special moments.

ACTION AND EMOTION RESPONSE

In relationships, how we respond to situations can significantly impact our interactions. Some of us are more action-oriented, while others are guided by emotions. Understanding these response styles can strengthen the bond between you and your partner by fostering empathy and improving communication.

Those who are action response-minded focus on what needs to be done. Their first instinct in any situation is to find a solution, take steps, and get things done. For instance, in my marriage, when a problem arises, my action-oriented side kicks in to immediately search for ways to fix it. I'm practical, task-oriented, and driven by results. For me, love and support are often expressed through actions—whether that's solving a problem, offering help, or taking tangible steps to make things better. My focus is on resolving the issue, ensuring things get back on track as quickly as possible.

On the other hand, emotion response-minded individuals center their attention on feelings. Their priority is to understand and address the emotional landscape of any situation, whether it's their own emotions or their partner's. Lauren, for example, often approaches problems by first wanting to talk about how it feels and what emotions are involved. She values empathy, understanding, and emotional connection. For her, love and support are shown through listening, comforting, and validating her partner's feelings, creating a sense of emotional safety and closeness before taking any further action.

When it comes to communication, action response-minded individuals typically prefer discussing solutions, planning actions, and focusing on what can be done to improve a situation. Their conversations often revolve around finding practical ways to move forward, and they may not spend much time dwelling on emotions. They feel most comfortable when there's a clear plan or solution in place. In contrast, emotion response-minded individuals are more focused on exploring feelings, discussing the emotional impacts of a situation, and ensuring that both partners feel understood. For them, conversations are about making sure both people are emotionally in tune before jumping into any action.

This difference becomes even more apparent in how conflicts are resolved. Action response-minded people tend to handle conflicts by immediately proposing solutions and taking steps to resolve the issue as quickly as possible. Their instinct is to fix the problem so that things can return to normal. On the other hand, emotion response-minded individuals often approach conflicts by expressing their feelings and seeking emotional resolution first. They want to be heard and understood emotionally before moving forward with any practical solutions. For them, the heart of conflict resolution lies in addressing the emotions behind the issue, not just the problem itself.

When it comes to emotional connection, action response-minded individuals often feel bonded through shared activities and problem-solving together. They believe that love is shown through tangible actions and working as a team to overcome challenges. In contrast, emotion response-minded individuals feel most connected when they share their emotions and experience empathetic listening from their partner. For them, emotional sharing and being understood on a deeper level create a sense of closeness and intimacy.

CLOSING SUMMARY

As we wrap up Chapter 1, it's clear that understanding the unique ways we think and respond is foundational to building strong, healthy relationships. Whether you identify more with a waffle mind or a spaghetti mind, or lean towards quantity or quality thinking, recognizing these differences is the first step toward deeper connection and mutual respect.

Lauren and I have experienced firsthand how our distinct approaches can both challenge and enrich our relationship. My methodical, action-oriented mindset complements Lauren's emotionally intuitive and holistic way of navigating our interactions. By embracing our individual styles, we've learned to bridge gaps, communicate more effectively, and support each other's needs in meaningful ways.

Remember, there’s no right or wrong way to think or respond in a relationship. It's all about understanding and appreciating each other's unique perspectives. With this understanding, you both can create a dynamic and supportive environment where love can truly flourish.

Marriage Tip

It's not about thinking like your spouse but understanding and accepting their different ways of thinking. Often, both perspectives can be right but see things differently.

CHAPTER 2: THE DIFFERENCES IN EMOTIONAL PROCESSING

When it comes to processing our emotions, there's a lot more happening beneath the surface than we might realize. A major part of how we handle our emotions is shaped by our upbringing. The way our parents raised us, how they dealt with emotions, and the environment we grew up in play a significant role in shaping our emotional responses as adults. If we were encouraged to express our feelings openly as children, we might feel more comfortable doing so in relationships. On the flip side, if we grew up in an environment where emotions were suppressed or ignored, we might struggle to express or even understand our own feelings as adults.

But it's not just our upbringing that influences how we process emotions. The joys and traumas we experienced during childhood and adolescence leave a lasting mark. Positive experiences can give us confidence in navigating emotions, while unresolved trauma can make it more difficult to manage our feelings in healthy ways. Additionally, our current physical and mental health plays a significant role in how we process emotions daily. Stress, fatigue, or mental health struggles can amplify our emotional reactions, while feeling balanced and healthy can make it easier to cope with emotional ups and downs.

Emotional processing isn't static—it evolves with our life experiences and personal growth. The way we handled emotions in our twenties may look very different from how we process them in our forties or beyond. As we encounter new challenges, successes, and changes, our emotional toolkit expands and adapts. What worked for us emotionally at one stage in life may not suffice as we grow older and face new situations.

Understanding these influences is crucial in relationships, especially during emotional highs and lows. By recognizing the many layers behind how we process emotions, we can approach our partner with greater empathy and patience. We realize that their emotional responses aren't just about the present moment but are shaped by a lifetime of experiences. This awareness allows us to offer more effective support and helps create a deeper emotional connection, fostering a stronger, more understanding relationship.

WAVE AND ICEBERG EMOTIONAL PROCESSING

In relationships, understanding how you and your partner process emotions can make a world of difference. Let's explore two styles: **Wave Processors** and **Iceberg Processors**. These analogies can help explain different approaches to handling intense moments.

Wave processors might initially appear unaffected or detached during an emotional situation, seeming ready to move on or make decisions quickly. However, this doesn't mean they aren't feeling anything. It simply takes time for their emotions to fully surface and for them to understand what they're feeling. Over time, these emotions come in gradually, and they'll need space to process and express their feelings more deeply later on.

In contrast, iceberg processors experience their emotions instantly and need to express them right away. They feel the full intensity of their feelings in the moment and have an urgent need for validation and understanding. For them, emotions are like an iceberg—massive and present immediately, requiring acknowledgment before they can let go or move forward. If they're unable to express themselves in real-time, they can feel stuck, as if they're frozen in place emotionally.

These emotional processing styles also impact communication. Wave processors often need time to gather their thoughts and fully understand what they're feeling before they're ready to talk about it. They might withdraw or seem distant initially, not because they don't care, but because they're still working through their emotions. If forced to engage in emotional conversations too soon, a wave processor can feel overwhelmed, triggering a fight-or-flight response. They might either shut down or lash out, leading to further misunderstandings.

On the other hand, iceberg processors find it difficult to wait for a discussion. They need to talk about their feelings immediately and seek emotional validation in the moment. For them, unresolved feelings feel unbearable, and they may push for an immediate conversation to release the emotional tension. If their partner isn't ready to engage, iceberg processors can feel abandoned or as though their heart is being held hostage. When emotions aren't addressed, it's like they're left emotionally paralyzed, unable to move on.

These differences become especially apparent during conflict resolution. Wave processors tend to revisit issues later on, once their emotions have caught up with the situation. What seemed resolved in the moment might resurface later as they gain clarity on their true feelings. They often need to process internally before they can re-engage and resolve lingering issues. Iceberg processors, on the other hand, push for immediate resolution. They need emotional acknowledgment right away to feel heard and validated. If left unresolved, they may struggle to move forward, feeling trapped by unexpressed emotions.

In marriage, these dynamics can lead to tension if partners don't understand each other's emotional processing styles. A wave processor's need for time and space may feel like avoidance or indifference to an iceberg processor, who is ready to address everything immediately. Likewise, an iceberg processor's urgency for emotional resolution may feel overwhelming to a wave processor, who simply isn't ready to engage yet. By understanding and respecting each other's needs, couples can create a balance that fosters both emotional safety and deeper connection.

Understanding how you and your partner process emotions is crucial for navigating the complexities of any relationship. Whether you lean toward the wave or iceberg style of emotional processing, recognizing these differences can prevent unnecessary conflict and foster deeper empathy. Waves need time to process and reflect, while icebergs need immediate emotional validation. When these distinct styles clash, it's easy to feel misunderstood, but with patience and mutual respect, you can create a relationship where both emotional needs are honored.

INFLUENCE OF UPBRINGING AND CHILDHOOD EXPERIENCES

Unvoiced emotional expectations can create a lot of tension and misunderstandings, and this is especially true in marriage. These unspoken expectations often stem from our childhood experiences and deeply affect how we relate to our partner. The silent needs we bring into relationships, often rooted in what we did or didn't receive as children, shape our emotional landscape. The key to navigating these hidden expectations is understanding both yourself and your partner, and being willing to communicate openly.

Think about the hopes and desires you carry into your relationship—things you may never have fully articulated, even to yourself. These expectations often center around emotional needs like affection, communication, support, or validation. If, for instance, you grew up in a home where affection was rarely expressed, you might now long for constant reassurance from your partner. Or perhaps, if you were constantly praised as a child, you may expect your partner to frequently validate your efforts and achievements. These emotional expectations are tricky because they're often unspoken. You may assume your partner knows what you need or expect them to naturally fulfill these desires without ever clearly communicating them. The problem arises when these needs go unmet, leading to disappointment and frustration. Without clear communication, your partner may have no idea they've fallen short of something you never fully expressed in the first place.

To break this cycle, self-understanding is crucial. Reflecting on your own childhood experiences can help you see how they influence your emotional needs and expectations today. What did you long for as a child that you might now seek from your partner? Did you crave more emotional support? Did you need more validation or affection? By identifying these patterns, you can start to recognize how they play out in your current relationship.

Once you understand your own expectations, the next step is to voice them. It's important to have open and honest conversations with your partner about what you need emotionally. Clear communication can make a world of difference, helping your partner understand you better and giving them the opportunity to meet your needs in ways they may not have known about before.

Just as you carry unvoiced expectations into your relationship, so does your partner. They, too, are shaped by their childhood experiences, and understanding their emotional landscape is just as important as understanding your own. Take time to learn about their background—what did they receive or lack growing up? What silent hopes might they be bringing into your relationship? Encourage your partner to share their emotional needs with you, and listen with empathy. Understanding their perspective can help you both navigate each other's expectations with greater compassion and care. When both partners take the time to understand each other's emotional histories, it becomes easier to meet each other's needs and strengthen the bond between you.

The process of understanding and voicing emotional expectations can be transformative for your relationship. To help you navigate this journey, here are some strategies that can make a real difference. First, practice self-reflection by taking the time to think about your own childhood experiences and how they've shaped your emotional expectations. Journaling your thoughts can help you identify any unspoken needs that you might not have been fully aware of. Next, engage in open communication with your partner. Have honest, vulnerable conversations about your emotional needs and encourage them to do the same. Make it a safe space where both of you can share without fear of judgment. Finally, approach these conversations with empathy and patience. Remember that both you and your partner are bringing your own emotional histories into the relationship. By being patient and understanding, you can create an environment where both of you feel supported and heard.

PRACTICAL ADVICE FOR COUPLES

Handling emotions in a relationship isn't just about understanding feelings—it's about being practical, too. We often forget how much our physical state can influence our emotional responses. We all know that feeling hungry, tired, or stressed can make us more irritable, impatient, and prone to arguments. By recognizing these triggers and taking proactive steps, couples can avoid unnecessary conflicts and approach discussions with a clearer, more balanced mindset.

Our physical state directly impacts how we process and react to emotions. When you're hungry, tired, or physically exhausted, your tolerance for frustration naturally decreases. Small irritations can feel magnified, and emotions tend to flare up more quickly. This is why it's so easy for a simple disagreement to escalate into an argument when you're not physically at your best. For example, think about the last time you snapped at your partner when you were hungry or exhausted—it likely wasn't the actual issue that upset you, but rather your depleted physical state.

Recognizing how your body feels in the moment is a practical way to prevent these unnecessary conflicts. If you're aware that hunger makes you irritable or fatigue makes it hard to think clearly, you can take steps to address these physical needs before diving into an important or emotionally charged conversation. For instance, if you're feeling hungry, grab a snack before engaging in a discussion that requires your full attention. If you're exhausted after a long day, it might be best to postpone the conversation until you're rested and better able to focus. By acknowledging and managing your physical state, you set yourself up for more productive and less emotionally driven interactions with your partner.

One simple yet powerful practice is to check in with yourself before entering a discussion, especially one that has the potential to become heated. Ask yourself: Am I hungry? Tired? Stressed? These physical factors can have a significant impact on how you handle the conversation. If you're not feeling your best, let your partner know. It's okay to say, "I'm feeling really tired right now—can we talk about this later when I can give it my full attention?" This small moment of self-awareness can prevent a lot of unnecessary conflict.

Recognizing these physical triggers in your partner can also be helpful. If you notice that your partner seems irritable or out of sorts, it could be that they're dealing with physical exhaustion or stress. Rather than jumping into a conversation when emotions are running high, suggest postponing it until both of you are in a better frame of mind. This creates a safer, calmer space for communication and helps avoid arguments that arise simply because someone isn't physically at their best.

Understanding the practical side of handling emotions goes a long way in strengthening your relationship. Here are a few strategies that can help you manage your emotions more effectively:

First, take care of your basic needs. Make sure you're eating well, getting enough rest, and finding time to relax. Meeting these basic needs will help reduce the likelihood of heightened emotions leading to conflict. If you know you're more prone to emotional reactions when you're tired or hungry, prioritize those needs before engaging in important conversations.

Next, pause and reflect. If you feel a surge of emotion coming on, take a moment to pause. Reflect on how you're feeling physically. Are you hungry, tired, or stressed? Giving yourself a few moments to breathe, grab a snack, or rest can help you calm down and approach the conversation with a clearer head.

Finally, schedule important conversations at times when both you and your partner are well-rested, not hungry, and free from distractions. Setting the stage for important discussions during times when you're both physically and mentally in a good place will help make the conversation more productive and less emotionally charged.

Handling emotions in a relationship isn't just about understanding your feelings but also recognizing the practical impact of physical states on your emotional responses. By taking care of basic needs, checking in with yourself and your partner, and scheduling important conversations when you're both in a better state of mind, you can reduce unnecessary conflicts and create a healthier space for communication. Practical strategies like these are essential tools for keeping your relationship balanced and emotionally secure.

CLOSING SUMMARY

As we conclude Chapter 2, it's evident that emotional processing plays a pivotal role in shaping our relationships. Our upbringing, childhood experiences, and current physical and mental health all influence how we handle our emotions. Understanding whether you and your partner are Wave Processors or Iceberg Processors helps in navigating emotional landscapes with empathy and patience.

Lauren and I have discovered that recognizing our distinct emotional processing styles has strengthened our bond. By reflecting on our own backgrounds and openly communicating our emotional needs, we've built a foundation of mutual respect and support.

Moreover, acknowledging the practical aspects of emotional management, such as recognizing physical triggers and prioritizing self-care, has helped us prevent unnecessary conflicts and maintain a balanced relationship. These strategies not only enhance our emotional connection but also ensure that we approach challenges with a clearer, more composed mindset.

Marriage Tip

Major life changes, such as having a baby, changing jobs, or moving, can significantly increase stress levels. It's important to be aware of these stressors and avoid making major decisions during these times. Instead, focus on supporting each other through the transition.

CHAPTER 3: THE DIFFERENCE IN LOVE LANGUAGES

Love can be wonderfully simple yet incredibly complex. In the early stages of a relationship, love often shows up as passion and excitement—those butterflies you get from just liking each other. This initial spark is exhilarating and can make everything seem effortless. But that's just one side of love. As the relationship matures, love evolves into something deeper and more nuanced.

A huge part of this deeper love is how we communicate. Effective communication is essential in expressing love and ensuring both partners feel valued and understood. However, we all communicate love a little differently. What feels loving and affirming to one person might not resonate the same way with another.

This is where understanding each other's love languages comes in. Each of us has a unique way of feeling and showing love, and recognizing these differences is key to a fulfilling relationship. It's like discovering a special code that, when used correctly, makes expressing love so much more meaningful and clear. By learning and speaking each other's love languages, you can bridge any gaps in communication and ensure that your expressions of love are truly felt and appreciated.

By embracing the complexity of love and learning to communicate effectively, you create a strong foundation for a lasting and fulfilling relationship. It's a continuous journey of discovering and adapting to each other's needs, ensuring that the love you share grows deeper and more resilient with time.

THE THEORY OF LOVE AND RESPECT

In relationships, understanding how we each experience love can make a world of difference. While everyone's needs are unique, many couples find that love is often received in two primary ways: through caring and through respect. Generally, women tend to feel most loved when they experience acts of caring and emotional support, while men often feel most loved when they experience respect and admiration from their partner. These core differences shape how each person feels valued and connected in the relationship.

Let's start with women, who typically feel loved through caring actions. Women often feel most valued when their partner is emotionally available, thoughtful, and nurturing. Simple acts of kindness, like offering support after a tough day, listening attentively, or surprising them with a small gesture, can make women feel cherished. It's not always about grand romantic gestures—sometimes it's the little things that matter most. When a partner shows genuine care and empathy, women feel seen and appreciated. These actions convey that their emotions and well-being are important, which strengthens their sense of connection and love.

For men, the feeling of being loved is often tied to respect. Men generally feel most valued when their efforts, opinions, and contributions are acknowledged and respected. Whether it's a compliment on something they've achieved or simply showing appreciation for their hard work, men feel loved when they are admired and supported. Respect, in this sense, isn't just about deference—it's about being seen as competent, capable, and worthy of admiration. Acknowledging a man's opinions, valuing his input, and speaking to him with affirmation and gratitude help him feel esteemed and secure in the relationship.

These differences in how love is received can significantly impact how couples relate to each other. When it comes to showing love, it's essential to tailor your actions to your partner's needs. For women, love is expressed through caring gestures—being emotionally present, offering a listening ear, and showing kindness in small, thoughtful ways. These actions make women feel nurtured and emotionally safe.

For men, love is often expressed through respect—showing appreciation, recognizing their hard work, and speaking with admiration. These gestures make men feel respected and valued.

In terms of communication, women often feel cared for when their partner is attentive and supportive in conversations. Being a good listener and showing genuine interest in their thoughts and feelings helps them feel emotionally connected. Men, however, often feel respected when their partner listens actively, values their opinions, and expresses gratitude for their contributions. For men, communication is a space where respect is demonstrated through acknowledgment and appreciation.

When couples experience conflict, these dynamics can become even more important. For women, feeling cared for during a disagreement can soften the emotional intensity. Compassion, understanding, and reassurance that they're valued even in tense moments can help women feel secure. On the other hand, for men, feeling respected during conflict is key. Addressing issues calmly, acknowledging their perspective, and maintaining respect in how disagreements are handled can prevent them from feeling undervalued or dismissed.

Balancing these differences in how love is experienced is essential for a healthy and fulfilling relationship. One of the first steps is becoming aware of how your partner receives love and putting in the effort to meet their needs. Recognizing that both caring and respect are vital to the relationship helps ensure that both partners feel valued and appreciated.

Open communication is also crucial. Couples should talk openly about how they feel most loved and what actions make them feel respected or cared for. Understanding each other's love languages can deepen the bond and make both partners feel more connected.

LOVE LANGUAGES

Love isn't one-size-fits-all, and we each have our own way of feeling loved and appreciated. This is where the concept of love languages comes in. There are five general love language categories, and to truly love your partner effectively, it's important to understand and communicate in their love language, not just your own. When you speak their love language, you're giving love in a way that resonates with them on a deeper level, strengthening your connection.

Let's take a closer look at these five love languages:

Words of Affirmation

People who have this love language feel most loved through words—whether it's praise, encouragement, or appreciation. Compliments, kind words, and positive affirmations mean the world to them. For someone with this love language, words carry a lot of emotional weight. In a relationship, if this is your partner's love language, you can show love by regularly affirming them with heartfelt words, whether spoken or written. Simple notes, text messages, or telling them directly how much you appreciate them can make a huge impact. What matters is that the words are genuine and specific to who they are and what they do.

Acts of Service

For those who speak this love language, actions speak louder than words. They feel most loved when their partner does things to help or support them, like taking care of chores, running errands, or performing small acts of kindness. These gestures show that their partner is thinking of them and is willing to make an effort on their behalf. In a relationship, if your partner's love language is acts of service, showing love through actions is key. Help out around the house, run an errand they've been dreading, or do something special to make their day a little easier. The gesture itself is a powerful message of love and support.

Receiving Gifts

People with this love language feel loved when they receive thoughtful gifts. It's not about the monetary value, but rather the thought and effort behind the gift that counts. A well-chosen, meaningful gift shows that their partner is paying attention to what they like and care about. If this is your partner's love language, surprising them with small, thoughtful gifts or gestures can go a long way. The gift doesn't have to be extravagant; it could be something as simple as bringing home their favorite snack or something that reminds them of a special memory. It's the act of giving that makes them feel cherished.

Quality Time

For those who have this love language, nothing says love like having undivided attention from their partner. Spending meaningful time together is what they cherish most. It's not just about being physically present but being mentally and emotionally engaged as well. In a relationship, if your partner's love language is quality time, prioritize spending uninterrupted time with them. Put away distractions, such as your phone or TV, and focus on being present. Whether you're having deep conversations or just enjoying a quiet moment together, the key is to give them your full attention.

Physical Touch

For people with this love language, physical touch is the primary way they feel loved. Hugs, kisses, holding hands, and other forms of physical affection are incredibly important to them. It's how they feel connected and secure in their relationship. If your partner's love language is physical touch, make sure to show your affection through physical closeness. Small gestures like holding their hand, giving them a hug, or sitting close to them can make a big difference in how they feel loved and supported.

Communicating Love Through Their Language

To love your partner in the way that speaks most to them, you need to understand their primary love language. Pay attention to how they express love to you—often, people show love in the way they want to receive it. Notice what makes them light up and feel appreciated.

Once you know their love language, adapt your approach to show love in ways that resonate deeply with them. Even if your love language is different, making an effort to speak their language can strengthen your bond and bring you closer.

Understanding and using your partner's love language consistently can transform your relationship. Here are a few strategies to help you incorporate their love language into your daily life:

First, observe and listen. Pay close attention to how your partner expresses love to you and what they seem to appreciate most in your relationship. Their actions and words may give you clues about their love language.

Second, have an open conversation. Share your own love language and ask about theirs. This mutual understanding will help both of you feel more loved and appreciated.

Finally, make it a habit. Love is best expressed through consistent actions, so try to make it a daily practice to show love in a way that resonates with them—whether it's through words, actions, gifts, time, or touch.

Understanding and speaking your partner's love language can be one of the most powerful ways to deepen your connection and ensure both of you feel valued and appreciated. By making the effort to communicate love in a way that resonates with them, you're building a stronger foundation for your relationship. It's about meeting each other's needs and embracing the differences that make your bond unique. Whether through words, acts of service, time, gifts, or touch, speaking the right love language can transform how you and your partner connect on a daily basis.

LOVE IS AN ACTION AND A CHOICE

In any romantic relationship, love goes far beyond just feelings—it's something you actively do, and it's a choice you make every single day. Think of it like tending a garden: flowers need regular care, just as love needs consistent nurturing to thrive.

Love isn't just about saying, "I love you"; it's about showing it in the everyday things we do. Whether it's surprising your partner with their favorite snack, taking the time to listen when they've had a rough day, or simply being present, these actions are how love comes to life. Big romantic gestures are great, but it's those small, consistent acts of kindness that truly keep a relationship strong. You wouldn't water a plant once and expect it to stay healthy forever, right? It's the same with love—it's the daily care that makes the difference.

Love is also a choice we make every day. It's choosing to be patient when you're frustrated, forgiving when you're hurt, or kind when you're tired. There will be days when love doesn't feel effortless, and that's when making the choice to love becomes so important. This choice is what keeps love intentional and active, even in the tough moments. Every time you choose to love, you're investing in the growth of your relationship—just like how you'd keep tending a garden to make sure it blooms.

Just like a flower doesn't thrive on one watering, love can't survive on a single grand gesture. A romantic weekend away or a heartfelt gift can feel amazing, but what really keeps a relationship going are the consistent, everyday actions. Think of it as hitting the refresh button on your love regularly. Without that ongoing effort, the relationship can wither. Keep the little moments of love alive, and you'll keep the relationship vibrant and strong.

Understanding that love is both an action and a choice can really change the way you approach your relationship. It doesn't take much to show love—sometimes, it's as simple as offering a genuine compliment, grabbing their hand when you're walking together, or sending a quick text to let them know you're thinking of them. These small, everyday gestures may seem insignificant, but they add up in ways that strengthen your connection over time.

There will also be days when choosing love feels harder. Maybe you're stressed, tired, or feeling frustrated. It's in those moments that love becomes a real choice. Deciding to respond with kindness, patience, or understanding—especially when it's tough—makes all the difference. It's those choices that keep love active and alive.

Love isn't something you can just set and forget. It requires ongoing effort. You have to continue finding new ways to connect and keep the relationship vibrant. This might be through shared activities, meaningful conversations, or simply spending quality time together. The key is to keep putting in the effort because your relationship is worth it.

Ultimately, love is something we actively nurture every day. It's not just the grand gestures that matter, but the small, consistent actions that build a strong foundation. By making love a choice in both the easy and difficult moments, we ensure that our relationships continue to grow and flourish. The effort we put in reflects the value we place on the relationship, and that ongoing care is what keeps love alive.

CLOSING SUMMARY

As we wrap up Chapter 3, it's clear that understanding each other's love languages is pivotal in building a strong and fulfilling relationship. Whether it's through caring gestures, words of affirmation, acts of service, quality time, or physical touch, recognizing how your partner feels most loved allows you to communicate love more effectively.

Lauren and I have experienced firsthand how speaking each other's love languages has deepened our connection and minimized misunderstandings. By tailoring our actions to meet each other's emotional needs, we've created a more harmonious and resilient relationship.

But love doesn't stop at understanding and speaking each other's love languages. It's also about recognizing that love is both an action and a choice. Just as Lauren and I make conscious decisions every day to nurture our relationship—whether that's setting aside quality time together, offering words of encouragement, or showing respect through our actions—we ensure that our love remains active and intentional. These consistent, everyday actions are the foundation that keeps our relationship vibrant and strong, much like tending to a garden ensures its continual growth and bloom.

Choosing to love actively means being present, patient, and willing to adapt to each other's evolving needs. It’s about making daily commitments to support and cherish one another, even when it's challenging. This proactive approach to love ensures that our bond not only survives but thrives through life's ups and downs.

By embracing both the love languages and the understanding that love is an ongoing action and choice, we build a relationship grounded in mutual respect, appreciation, and deep emotional connection. This dual approach fosters a love that is both profound and enduring, capable of weathering any storm and celebrating every joy together.

Marriage Tip

Apology Languages: Just as with love languages, people have different ways they prefer to receive apologies. Understanding these can make apologies more effective and sincere. Common apology languages include expressing regret, accepting responsibility, making restitution, genuinely repenting, and requesting forgiveness.

SECTION 2: COMMUNICATING CLEAR EXPECTATIONS & GROWING A MINDSET OF ADAPTATION

Every relationship will face change, and it's how we adapt and communicate through those changes that either brings us closer or pushes us apart. Most arguments don't happen because of huge, insurmountable problems—they stem from misunderstandings, unspoken expectations, and the frustrations that follow. We often assume our partner knows what we want or need, but the truth is, none of us are mind-readers. Learning to clearly communicate what we expect and being open to our partner's expectations can save a lot of unnecessary conflict.

Think about it: how many times have you found yourself frustrated because something didn't go the way you expected, but you never really talked about those expectations beforehand? It happens to all of us. We get caught up in our own heads and forget that our partner might have a completely different perspective. That's why it's so important to get into the habit of talking openly about your needs, desires, and the changes that come up in life.

Life is constantly shifting—whether it's career changes, financial stresses, or new family dynamics—and the way you handle these changes as a couple makes a huge difference. The goal is to create a mindset where both of you can adapt together. It's not about one person bending entirely to fit the other's expectations, but rather both of you growing and evolving as a team. When you approach things with flexibility and clear communication, you're setting yourselves up to face life's twists and turns without losing connection.

We'll also dive into some of the more practical aspects of this, like managing money as a team and planning for the future. Finances can be one of the biggest sources of tension in relationships, especially if expectations around spending, saving, or budgeting aren't clear. That's why it's crucial to have open, honest conversations about how you want to manage your resources together. Life planning is another area where clear communication is key. As you both grow and your priorities shift, it's important to revisit your goals and adjust your plans as needed.

By identifying those moments when you need to recalibrate and discussing them openly, you'll find that you can navigate life's changes with far less friction. It's all about learning to grow together, communicate with love, and handle whatever life throws your way as a team. Through this process, you'll not only deepen your understanding of each other but also build a stronger, more resilient relationship.

CHAPTER 4: CLEAR EXPECTATIONS

As we've explored before, everyone has their own way of communicating and expressing love. With these differences come a set of expectations we naturally bring into our relationships. These expectations aren't inherently bad—in fact, they're an important and healthy part of any partnership. They help us understand what we need from one another. The problem arises when these expectations go unspoken. Often, it's not that our expectations are unreasonable, but simply that they haven't been communicated clearly. And that's where frustration or conflict can start to creep in.

We all have a tendency to assume that our partner knows what we want or need. It feels natural to think that because they know us so well, they should just "get" what we expect. But the truth is, unless we talk about those expectations openly, they may have no idea. We all have different backgrounds, experiences, and perspectives that shape how we see things, and what seems obvious to one person might not even cross the other's mind. This disconnect can lead to feelings of disappointment or even resentment when expectations go unmet, and that can easily snowball into bigger issues.

But it doesn't have to be that way. The key to avoiding these situations is getting comfortable with discussing your expectations early and often. It might feel a little awkward or uncomfortable at first—after all, no one wants to feel like they're demanding too much or coming across as needy. But the reality is that open conversations about what you both want and need are essential to keeping your relationship running smoothly. The more comfortable you get with these conversations, the less likely misunderstandings are to occur.

Having regular conversations about your expectations isn't about making demands or issuing ultimatums. It's about creating a safe and open space where both of you can express your thoughts and feelings freely. When you're able to communicate your expectations clearly, you're not only preventing conflicts but also ensuring that both partners feel heard, valued, and supported. This kind of transparency fosters trust and strengthens the bond between you. It allows both of you to thrive because you're able to meet each other's needs in a way that feels authentic and caring.

Ultimately, a relationship where expectations are openly discussed is one where both people can grow and feel secure. When you know what your partner needs from you—and when they know what you need from them—it builds a foundation of mutual respect and understanding. And that's where real connection happens.

LEARNING WHAT TO EXPECT

A lot of the expectations we bring into relationships come from our childhood experiences. These early influences shape what we imagine our partner's roles should be, often without us even realizing it. For example, someone who grew up in a traditional home might have very different expectations than someone raised in a more progressive environment. That's why it's so important to take time to sit down and talk with each other about how you view your roles in the relationship. Are you on the same page, or are there areas where you might need to adjust those expectations?

The way we were raised has a powerful influence on how we see spousal roles. If you grew up in a home where certain responsibilities were divided based on gender, those expectations can become deeply ingrained. You might think a husband or wife is supposed to behave in a certain way or take on specific tasks. But in a relationship, these unspoken assumptions can easily lead to misunderstandings. For instance, if one person expects traditional roles and the other wants to share tasks more equally, it can create tension that neither of you anticipated.

If you were raised in a more traditional setting, you might expect clear and defined roles for each partner—like the idea that certain tasks belong to one person exclusively. On the other hand, if you come from a progressive background, you might expect a more fluid approach, with responsibilities being shared and decisions made together. Neither perspective is right or wrong, but if you don't talk about these expectations, it can lead to frustration.

This is where communication becomes crucial. You and your partner need to openly share how your upbringing has shaped your views on these roles. Talk about your expectations and really listen to each other's perspectives without judgment. By having these conversations, you'll start to see where your views align and where they differ. This understanding allows you to make conscious decisions about how to structure your roles in a way that works for both of you.

Once you've had these open conversations, you may realize that some adjustments need to be made. That's okay. Being willing to compromise is a sign of growth. The goal is to create roles and responsibilities that fit your unique relationship—not simply to follow the model you grew up with. You might find a balance that blends both traditional and progressive elements in a way that suits you both. The key is to make it your own and ensure it works for the relationship you're building together.

By understanding how your upbringing has shaped your expectations, you can approach your relationship with more clarity and empathy. Communicating openly about roles and responsibilities helps you avoid misunderstandings and allows both of you to feel heard and respected. It's not about holding on to past patterns, but about creating a new path that works for your unique partnership. By being willing to listen, compromise, and redefine roles, you're setting the foundation for a relationship that's built on mutual understanding and shared growth.

TALK ABOUT THE HARD THINGS EARLY

In any relationship, addressing the hard topics early on can make all the difference. While these conversations might feel uncomfortable at first, getting them out in the open builds a foundation of trust and understanding. Talking about key issues such as sex, date nights, kids, politics, religion, work, friendships, social media, passwords, and money handling early in the relationship can prevent misunderstandings and conflicts down the road.

Having these conversations early on helps both of you set clear expectations, reducing the chance of future conflict. By being transparent and honest, you foster trust and ensure that both partners feel heard. Let's break down some of these critical areas:

Sex

Sex is often a sensitive topic, but openly discussing it can prevent a lot of future tension. Be clear about your expectations around intimacy, including how frequently you'd like to have sex. For example, discuss whether having sex a couple of times a week feels ideal, or if a less frequent schedule, like once or twice a month, works better. By understanding each other's desires and needs, you create a more respectful and fulfilling sexual relationship.

Date Nights

Date nights are another essential area to discuss. Decide together how often you want to prioritize time for just the two of you and what kinds of activities you both enjoy. Whether it's weekly or monthly, having these moments helps keep the connection strong and reinforces your bond.

Kids and Parenting

When it comes to kids, it's important to talk not just about whether you want children and how many, but also about your approach to parenting. This includes discussing discipline methods such as spankings, timeouts, and teaching manners. Do you both agree on using timeouts, or would you prefer a gentler approach? How do you feel about spankings or other methods of discipline? Aligning your views on how to raise children helps ensure consistency and avoids future disagreements.

Lauren and I spent a lot of time discussing our parenting philosophies. Understanding each other's perspectives early on helped us create a unified approach that works for both of us, making us feel more confident, unified and prepared for the challenges of parenting together.

Politics and Religion

Politics can be another area of potential conflict. Sharing your political views and talking about how you plan to handle differences of opinion is essential. Respecting each other's perspectives, even if you don't always agree, creates space for a healthier relationship.

Religion and church involvement can also play a big role in your lives. Talk about your religious beliefs, how you practice your faith, and what role you want the church to play in your relationship and family life. Understanding each other's spiritual needs will help you offer mutual support, even if you come from different backgrounds.

Work and Career Goals

Work is another important topic to cover. Discuss your career goals, how you'll balance work and personal life, and how you'll support each other's ambitions. Knowing how work fits into your relationship ensures that both of you feel valued in your personal and professional growth.

Friendships and Boundaries

Friendships, particularly opposite-sex friendships, are also worth discussing. Talk about how you approach boundaries in these friendships and ensure both of you feel comfortable. Building trust in these areas helps prevent unnecessary tension.

We've had open conversations about our friendships, setting clear boundaries that respect each other's comfort levels. This transparency has helped us maintain healthy friendships without feeling threatened or insecure.

Social Media and Privacy

With social media becoming such a big part of modern relationships, it's important to discuss your boundaries around its use. This could include whether or not you want to share passwords, how transparent you want to be online, and how you each view privacy. By talking through these issues, you can prevent future misunderstandings.

Money Handling

When it comes to money handling, discussing whether to have shared or separate bank accounts is key. Some couples prefer to pool all their resources into joint accounts, while others find it easier to keep things separate. Whatever your approach, talking about budgeting, saving, and spending early on ensures that financial stress doesn't become a source of conflict later.

Embracing Tough Conversations

Having these tough conversations early on might feel uncomfortable at first, but they are crucial for building a relationship that's grounded in trust and openness. Be honest, listen without judgment, and make sure to revisit these topics regularly as your relationship grows and evolves. Addressing the hard things early will set you up for a relationship built on mutual respect, understanding, and long-term success.

EMOTIONAL AWARENESS

In any relationship, especially in marriage, emotions can sometimes get the best of us, even when we're trying our hardest to communicate clearly. When you're discussing expectations, it's natural for feelings to run high—especially if the conversation touches on sensitive topics. If frustration starts to build, it's important to pause and remind each other that you're both on the same team. A simple "I love you" or a reassuring touch can make all the difference, helping you reset and refocus on the conversation.

Managing emotions is key to having productive discussions. It's easy for frustration, anger, or hurt to creep in, derailing the conversation and leading to misunderstandings. The best way to handle these emotional spikes is to recognize when they're happening and take a step back. If things start to get heated, it's okay to pause. Taking a few deep breaths or even stepping away for a moment can help you both calm down and come back to the conversation with clearer heads. Staying grounded in your love and commitment to each other can diffuse tension and reinforce the fact that you're working towards the same goal.

One of the most important things to remember is that you and your partner are on the same team. You're not adversaries, and disagreements aren't battles to win.

Instead, you're partners working together to build a stronger, more loving relationship. Keeping this "team mindset" in mind can shift the focus from the disagreement to your shared goals and values. Even when you don't see eye-to-eye, you both ultimately want the same thing: a healthy, happy relationship.

One way to manage emotions during difficult conversations is to regularly check in with each other. Asking how your partner is feeling, and being honest about your own emotions, helps keep the conversation grounded. If things get too intense, taking a short break is another good strategy. Stepping away for just a few minutes can give you both the space to cool down and gather your thoughts. And when expressing your feelings, try to use "I" statements, like "I feel overwhelmed," instead of "You're overwhelming me." This approach helps keep the focus on your own emotions without placing blame or causing your partner to feel defensive.

CLOSING SUMMARY

As we conclude Chapter 4, it's evident that clear expectations are fundamental to a healthy and harmonious relationship. Whether these expectations stem from our upbringing, personal experiences, or individual needs, the key to managing them lies in open and honest communication. By discussing your expectations early and regularly, you prevent misunderstandings and build a foundation of trust and mutual respect.

Lauren and I have learned that openly sharing our expectations—from household roles to financial management and beyond—has been instrumental in maintaining our strong connection. These conversations have not only clarified our individual needs but have also allowed us to support each other in meaningful ways. By addressing the hard topics early, we've avoided many potential conflicts and ensured that our relationship remains resilient and fulfilling.

Moreover, emotional awareness plays a crucial role in how we handle these discussions. Recognizing and managing our emotions ensures that even when conversations become intense, we can navigate them with patience and understanding. This emotional intelligence strengthens our bond and reinforces our commitment to working together as a team.

Marriage Tip

Misunderstandings are common. Avoid assuming your spouse is intentionally trying to hurt you. Always opt for open dialogue.

CHAPTER 5: LIFE APPLICATIONS

With all the different expectations a couple navigates, there are some subjects that carry more weight than others. Three of the most significant are money, children, and time-management. These areas can make or break a relationship, no matter how deeply you love each other. It's not that love isn't important—it absolutely is—but these topics are fundamental to your daily life and your long-term happiness together. They go beyond affection and touch on your values, priorities, and how you envision your future as a couple.

These areas—money, children, and time-management—can create misunderstandings or foster resentment if left unaddressed. But by tackling these topics head-on, you give yourselves the opportunity to grow stronger together. Open, honest discussions help you understand each other's perspectives and work through any challenges with clarity and intention. It doesn't matter if you're newlyweds or if you've been together for years—regularly revisiting these subjects will help you stay connected and aligned as you evolve and grow.

Ultimately, it's about building a relationship where you feel secure and supported, knowing that you're both moving in the same direction. When you approach these heavier subjects with openness and mutual respect, you're laying a solid foundation for a partnership that can withstand the ups and downs of life. It's not always easy, but it's worth it when the result is a stronger, more resilient relationship that continues to thrive over time.

MONEY IN MARRIAGE

Money can quickly become one of the biggest sources of tension in a relationship, especially in marriage. It's not unusual for couples to have very different views on money—just like they might have different thoughts about many other aspects of life. Whether it's about how to spend, save, or invest, these differences can lead to conflicts if not managed properly. That's why it's so important to have clear conversations about your financial goals, expectations, and habits from the start. When issues arise, it's essential to talk about them openly and work together to adapt.

Just like other parts of your relationship, you and your partner likely have different perspectives on money. These differences can stem from how you were raised, personal experiences with money, or simply individual values. Maybe one of you tends to save, while the other likes to spend more freely. These opposing habits can create tension if not addressed directly. If left unchecked, they can lead to misunderstandings, frustration, and even resentment.

The key to navigating this is to have clear, honest conversations. Talk openly about how you each approach money—your spending habits, saving strategies, and long-term goals. Discuss what's important to you financially. Do you want to save for a house, take regular vacations, or build up retirement savings? It's important to be upfront about what you expect from each other when it comes to finances. By establishing a mutual understanding and setting clear expectations, you can avoid many of the conflicts that arise from financial miscommunication.

But even with the best planning, financial problems will come up. When that happens, it's crucial not to let these issues fester. Address them directly by talking about the problem calmly and constructively. The goal is to solve the issue together, not to blame each other. Financial plans may need to change over time—whether because of a job loss, an unexpected expense, or simply a shift in priorities. The ability to adapt and make adjustments is key to managing money effectively as a team. Flexibility is just as important as the plans you make.

There are a few practical strategies that can help keep things on track when it comes to handling money in your marriage. First, schedule regular financial check-ins. Whether it's weekly or monthly, sitting down together to go over your finances ensures that both of you are informed and involved. This can help you avoid any surprises down the road. Creating a budget together is another helpful tool. A budget that reflects both of your priorities and goals allows for more realistic financial planning and flexibility when needed. Setting joint goals—like saving for a home, a dream vacation, or retirement—helps strengthen your partnership, giving you something to work towards together.

Perhaps most importantly, respect each other's views on money. Acknowledge that your partner might see things differently, and find compromises that honor both of your perspectives. Money doesn't have to be a source of division—it can be something you manage together as a team.

Clear communication around money not only strengthens your financial partnership but also helps build trust and mutual respect in your relationship. By tackling financial challenges together, you create a stronger bond that allows you both to grow, adapt, and feel secure. The more you work as a team in managing your finances, the more harmony and connection you'll experience across all areas of your life together.

Money Handling Tip

Talk about how you want to handle your bank accounts and bills. You can still have your personal accounts and a joint account, with both of you being signers on all of them.

Try using math and percentages to break down the amounts in a way that feels fair to both of you. Set spending limits for amounts that need a conversation before purchasing. For example, maybe you both agree that anything under $200 doesn't need to be discussed.

One of you might be a spender while the other is a saver. One might be a nerd when it comes to finances, and the other a free spirit. It's important to understand how each of you views and uses money, and then learn to work together on it.

CHILDREN

When it comes to marriage, children are one of the biggest topics that require ongoing conversation. As parents, you and your partner will likely have different ideas on nearly everything—discipline, education, recreation, safety, screen time, doctor visits, babysitters, sleepovers, and more. It's natural to have differing opinions because you both come from unique backgrounds and experiences that shape your views on parenting. The goal isn't about being right or wrong but rather about finding ways to work together in raising your children with love, respect, and understanding.

Your different perspectives on how to raise children can sometimes lead to conflicts if they're not addressed openly. One of you might have a more discipline-focused approach, while the other prioritizes nurturing. These differences don't have to create division; in fact, in some situations, one approach might be more appropriate than the other. It's not always about one style being right or wrong—it's about recognizing that each situation might call for a different approach. Part of this process is learning to trust each other's instincts and respecting that both of you are navigating parenting together, often learning as you go.

The key to managing these differences is constant communication. Have regular, open discussions about your parenting philosophies and approaches. The more you talk, the better you'll understand where your partner is coming from, and vice versa. These conversations aren't just one-time discussions—they're ongoing, as your children grow and as new challenges arise. Make sure to clearly outline your expectations for things like discipline, education, or even screen time, so you can prevent misunderstandings and stay on the same page.

When you approach parenting as a team, you're not just managing conflicts—you're building a stronger relationship with each other and with your children. It's not about one person being right and the other wrong. Instead, focus on working together in a way that respects both of your perspectives. The key to success in parenting is flexibility and the willingness to compromise. Sometimes you'll need to find a middle ground where both of you feel heard and your children's needs are prioritized. Trust in each other's ability to handle certain situations, knowing that parenting is a process of continuous learning.

Some practical strategies can help ensure that you're both involved in parenting decisions. First, schedule regular parenting meetings. These don't have to be formal, but setting aside time to discuss your parenting approaches and any concerns that come up will help keep both of you informed and engaged. It's also helpful to create parenting plans. These plans can cover topics like discipline, screen time, education, and even how you want to handle family rules. Keep these plans flexible and open to change, as parenting requires constant adaptation.

Supporting each other's parenting styles is also crucial. Even if you don't always agree on every decision, showing a united front helps provide your children with a stable and consistent environment. Finally, respect each other's views on parenting. By acknowledging your partner's perspective and finding compromises that reflect both of your needs, you'll create a more harmonious home life. Trust that both of you are working towards the same goal and learning together as you raise your children.

Parenting requires constant communication, trust, and flexibility. By recognizing that different situations call for different approaches and by learning to trust each other's instincts, you can work together to raise your children with greater harmony and understanding. Parenting as a team strengthens not only your relationship with your children but also with each other, as you navigate the complexities of parenthood together.

Parenting Tip

You have to learn how to trust each other. Parenting is incredibly unique and changes from situation to situation. There will be moments where one parent's preferred method or idea will work best and other moments where the other parent's seemingly opposite methods and ideas will work best. You need to learn how to trust and discern within each moment.

TIME MANAGEMENT

In any relationship, time management is crucial. Depending on where you are in life, you might find yourselves spending every second together, or you might feel like you barely see each other. As life changes, so will your availability. Whether it's due to new jobs, kids, or other responsibilities, you'll need to adapt to these changes by learning how to prioritize and make time for what truly matters. As you grow, it's important to recognize when to say yes and when to say no to commitments that demand your time.

Life is always shifting, and your free time will likely shift with it. New jobs, expanding families, or additional responsibilities can quickly eat up the time you once had together. This is why it's so important to manage your time effectively as a couple. Even when life gets hectic, you need to be intentional about carving out moments for each other. Time together is not just a luxury—it's an essential part of keeping your relationship strong and connected. Adapting to these changes with flexibility and focus helps ensure that your relationship doesn't get lost in the shuffle.

Lauren and I have faced this firsthand. When we first had our child, finding time for each other was incredibly challenging. We had to be creative in scheduling date nights (even at home) and ensure that we were present during the moments we did have together. It took effort, but it was worth it to keep our connection strong amidst the demands of parenthood.

Prioritizing what's important becomes more vital as your life fills up with responsibilities. You both need to figure out what matters most—whether it's spending time together, working on shared goals, or supporting each other's personal growth. This might mean actively scheduling date nights, planning time for activities you both enjoy, or setting aside moments for meaningful conversations. The key is to not let life's demands crowd out what truly matters in your relationship.

One of the most valuable lessons you'll learn as you mature is how to say yes and no when it comes to your time. Not every demand on your schedule deserves your attention. It's important to recognize where your time is best spent and make thoughtful decisions about what you can realistically commit to. Balancing your commitments helps prevent overwhelm and burnout. Whether it's work, family, friends, or personal interests, you need to manage how you allocate your time so that you're both maintaining balance and nurturing your relationship.

A few practical strategies can help you manage your time more effectively as a couple. First, having regular check-ins about your schedules ensures that both of you are aware of each other's priorities. These conversations help you support each other and adjust as needed. Using a shared calendar can also be a lifesaver when it comes to staying organized. It helps you keep track of important dates, activities, and commitments, ensuring that you don't miss out on key moments together.

It's also important to be intentional about spending quality time together, even if it's just for a few minutes each day. Making sure that you're regularly connecting with each other, whether through a meaningful conversation, shared meal, or activity, nurtures your relationship in the midst of life's busyness. Additionally, regularly evaluating your commitments as a couple helps you focus on what truly matters. Together, you can decide what to prioritize and what to let go of, reducing stress and focusing on the things that bring the most value to your relationship.

Managing your time effectively is a crucial part of maintaining a healthy relationship. As life gets busier, it's important to prioritize what truly matters and create space for meaningful connection. By regularly checking in with each other, setting shared goals, and being intentional about how you spend your time, you ensure that your relationship continues to grow amidst the demands of everyday life. Learning to say no when necessary and focusing on what brings the most value to your partnership helps keep stress at bay and strengthens your bond.

Marriage Tip

Plan together to ensure you're prioritizing what's important to both of you. Don't neglect times of intimacy and make it a priority to have quality time with one another.

CLOSING SUMMARY

As we conclude Chapter 5, it's clear that life applications—specifically managing money, children, and time—are fundamental to maintaining a healthy and fulfilling relationship. These areas touch on core aspects of your daily life and long-term happiness together, requiring open communication, mutual respect, and strategic planning.

Lauren and I have learned that by addressing these significant topics head-on, we can prevent misunderstandings and build a stronger, more resilient partnership. Whether it's setting financial goals, aligning our parenting philosophies, or managing our time effectively, these conversations have been instrumental in keeping our relationship harmonious and thriving.

Moreover, navigating these life applications with empathy and flexibility ensures that both partners feel supported and valued. It’s about creating a partnership where both of you can grow individually and together, adapting to life's inevitable changes with a unified approach.

CHAPTER 6: LEARNING TO ADAPT

In any romantic relationship, even when you've put a lot of effort into communicating your expectations, it's important to remember that things change. What worked in one season of your life might not work in the next. Life is full of surprises—new jobs, the arrival of children, moving to a new city, or simply growing and evolving as individuals. These changes can shift the dynamics of your relationship and alter the roles you each play.

That's why being flexible and willing to adapt is so crucial. Making your expectations an ongoing conversation isn't just helpful—it's essential. It's not enough to discuss things once and assume they'll stay the same forever. Instead, make it a habit to regularly check in with each other about how you're feeling, what you need, and whether your current roles and responsibilities are still working for both of you.

Think of your relationship as a journey, not a destination. By staying adaptable and communicative, you can navigate life's changes together, maintaining a strong, supportive, and loving connection through all the different seasons of life.

Remember, it's normal for relationships to evolve over time. Embracing change rather than resisting it can lead to deeper understanding and a more resilient bond. So let's dive into how you can learn to adapt and grow together, turning challenges into opportunities to strengthen your relationship.

ADAPTING TO LIFE CHANGES

In any romantic relationship, big life transitions—like moving to a new place, changing careers, welcoming a child into your lives, or coping with the loss of a loved one—can shake things up in ways you might not expect. These events don't just alter your daily routines; they can touch every aspect of your lives together, from your emotional well-being to how you connect with each other. That's why it's so important to talk openly about whether you need to make any changes to your lifestyles or expectations.

Imagine you've just moved to a new city for one partner's job. Suddenly, you're both navigating unfamiliar streets, meeting new people, and perhaps dealing with feelings of homesickness. The partner who moved for their job might be diving into a demanding new role, while the other might be searching for their own new opportunities or adjusting to a different routine. In times like these, it's easy for misunderstandings or frustrations to arise if you're not communicating effectively.

That's where open and honest conversations come in. Sit down together and share how these changes are affecting each of you. Maybe one of you is feeling overwhelmed and needs more support around the house, or perhaps you're both craving more quality time together to reconnect amidst the chaos. By expressing your thoughts and listening to each other, you can start to understand how your current lifestyle fits—or doesn't fit—with your new circumstances.

Flexibility becomes your best friend during these transitions. Be willing to adjust your daily routines, shift responsibilities, or even rethink some of your long-term plans. It's not about sacrificing your needs but finding a new balance that works for both of you. Perhaps you agree to share household chores differently, or you set aside specific times each week to focus on each other without distractions.

Life transitions also offer an opportunity to revisit your expectations for your relationship. What you expected from each other before might not align with where you are now, and that's okay. The key is to recognize this and be open to adapting. Maybe you thought you'd always handle finances a certain way, but now one of you wants to take a more active role. Or perhaps the way you show affection needs to evolve as you both grow and change.

So how do you navigate these big changes together? Start by making communication a regular habit. Instead of waiting for frustrations to boil over, check in with each other frequently. Ask open-ended questions like, "How are you feeling about everything that's going on?" or "Is there anything I can do to support you better?" These conversations can help you catch small issues before they become big problems.

Working together to create a plan can also make a huge difference. If you're both clear on what needs to change and how you're going to tackle it, you'll feel more in control. Maybe you decide to set up a shared calendar to keep track of new responsibilities, or you agree to try out new ways of dividing tasks at home.

Don't forget that it's perfectly okay—and sometimes really helpful—to seek support outside your relationship. Talking to friends or family members who have been through similar experiences can provide valuable insights. If you're finding it particularly tough, consider reaching out to a professional who can offer guidance tailored to your situation.

Above all, make a conscious effort to stay connected. Life changes can be stressful, but they're also an opportunity to grow closer if you face them together. Plan date nights, take walks together, or find little moments in the day to check in with each other. These small acts can reinforce your bond and remind you both that you're a team navigating life together.

Remember, change is one of the few constants in life. Embracing it together can strengthen your relationship in ways you might not have imagined. By being flexible, communicating openly, and supporting each other, you can turn life's inevitable twists and turns into opportunities for deeper connection and mutual growth.

EMOTIONAL CHANGES

In every relationship, it's important to recognize that both partners will experience different emotional phases. Even when life seems stable and there's no major upheaval, one of you might find yourself feeling more emotional than usual—perhaps grappling with sadness, confusion, or a sense of being stuck. These periods are a natural part of life and offer an opportunity to show extra care and support for your partner.

Just as the seasons change, so do our inner emotional landscapes. There are times when everything feels bright and full of promise, and other moments when challenges weigh heavier on our hearts. Being mindful of these shifts in your partner can make a significant difference. Noticing when they're going through a tough time allows you to offer understanding and compassion when they need it most.

Supporting a partner during an emotional season involves being present and attentive. It might mean offering a listening ear without judgment, providing comforting words, or simply being there in silence. Show them that their feelings are valid and that you're there to navigate this period together. Sometimes, knowing they're not alone can be incredibly reassuring.

During these times, you may need to adjust your expectations and daily routines. Recognize that your partner might not have the capacity to handle all their usual responsibilities. Stepping in to help with tasks or easing certain pressures can alleviate some of their stress. Small acts of kindness—like preparing a favorite meal or taking care of chores unasked—can go a long way in showing your support.

Open communication remains key. Make it a habit to check in with each other about how you're feeling emotionally. Ask genuine questions like, "How are you really doing today?" and be prepared to listen. Sharing your own feelings can also encourage your partner to open up, fostering a deeper connection between you.

Creating a safe and accepting environment is crucial. Let your partner know that it's okay to express their emotions freely, without fear of criticism or dismissal. This mutual understanding can strengthen your bond and make it easier to face challenges together.

If the emotional difficulties become overwhelming, seeking professional help can be a valuable step. Therapists or counselors can provide guidance and tools to help both of you navigate these complex feelings more effectively.

Remember, being there for each other during emotional highs and lows enriches your relationship. By offering support and understanding when one of you is struggling, you build a foundation of trust and resilience. These shared experiences not only help you grow individually but also deepen the connection you share, turning challenges into opportunities for greater intimacy and mutual growth.

DO YOUR BEST AND FORGET THE REST

In any romantic relationship, it's vital to remember that both you and your partner are doing your best—even if some days that "best" looks different than others. Life has a way of throwing curveballs—stress at work, personal struggles, or just one of those days when nothing seems to go right. Recognizing that both of you are navigating your own challenges fosters a deeper sense of compassion and patience. Your relationship is a living, evolving connection that requires ongoing care and attention. The way you nurture it will naturally change over time, and adapting to these shifts is essential to keep your bond strong and healthy.

Think about the times when you've felt overwhelmed or not quite yourself. Maybe you're juggling multiple responsibilities, or perhaps you're just having an off day. Your energy might be lower, and you might not be as present as you'd like to be. The same goes for your partner. By acknowledging that each of you has these moments, you create space for understanding rather than frustration. It's about offering grace to one another and accepting that perfection isn't the goal—genuine effort and mutual support are.

Appreciating each other's efforts, no matter how big or small, creates a supportive environment where both partners feel seen and valued. It's easy to get caught up in our own perspectives and forget that our partner might be dealing with their own set of challenges. A simple "I appreciate you" or "Thanks for doing that" can go a long way in reinforcing your connection. These expressions of gratitude remind your partner that their efforts matter and that you're a team navigating life together.

Consider your relationship as a garden that thrives with regular care. This doesn't mean grand gestures all the time; often, it's the consistent, everyday acts of kindness that make the biggest difference. Whether it's making a cup of coffee for your partner in the morning, sending a thoughtful text during the day, or taking the time to listen when they need to talk, these small moments of connection nourish your relationship.

As you both grow and evolve, the needs of your relationship will change. What brought you joy and connection in the early days might look different now. Perhaps you once bonded over late-night adventures, and now you find fulfillment in quiet evenings at home. Being open to these changes and willing to adapt keeps your relationship dynamic and responsive to both of your needs.

Adapting doesn't mean losing yourself or compromising your values. It's about growing together and finding new ways to support and delight each other. Life events like career changes, personal goals, or family responsibilities can shift the balance in your relationship. By communicating openly and adjusting your expectations, you ensure that you're both on the same page and can navigate these changes smoothly.

So how can you embrace the mindset of doing your best and forgetting the rest? Start by regularly expressing appreciation for your partner's efforts. Let them know you notice and value what they bring to the relationship. Practice patience when things don't go as planned, understanding that setbacks are a natural part of life. Keep the lines of communication open—talk about how you're feeling and invite your partner to share as well. If something isn't working, discuss how you might adjust your approach together.

It's also important to let go of the need for perfection—both in yourself and in your partner. Unrealistic expectations can create unnecessary tension and disappointment. Instead, focus on the progress you're making and celebrate your successes, no matter how small. By accepting each other's imperfections, you create a safe space where genuine connection can flourish.

Letting go of what you can't control reduces stress and allows you to invest your energy where it counts. You can't control every outcome, but you can control how you respond and how you support each other. This shift in perspective enables you to face challenges with resilience and optimism, strengthening your relationship in the process.

At the heart of it, embracing the philosophy of "do your best and forget the rest" is about cultivating compassion and flexibility within your relationship. It's understanding that both you and your partner are imperfect beings doing your utmost amidst life's unpredictability. By committing to give your best each day and releasing the need to control every outcome, you foster a partnership grounded in empathy, patience, and mutual respect.

This mindset encourages you to focus on what truly matters—the love and connection you share—rather than getting bogged down by unmet expectations or external pressures. It invites you to appreciate the journey you're on together, with all its twists and turns, and to find joy in the growth and learning that come from navigating life's challenges side by side.

By doing your best and letting go of the rest, you create a nurturing environment where your relationship can thrive. You allow space for both of you to be authentically yourselves, supporting each other through the highs and lows. This approach not only strengthens your bond but also enriches your individual lives, enabling you to face the future with confidence, together.

CLOSING SUMMARY

As we conclude Chapter 6, it's evident that learning to adapt is fundamental to maintaining a strong and resilient relationship. Life is unpredictable, and the ability to navigate its changes with flexibility and open communication can make all the difference. Whether you're facing major transitions like moving cities or welcoming a child, or simply dealing with everyday emotional shifts, adapting together ensures that your bond remains unshaken.

Lauren and I have discovered that by staying adaptable—regularly checking in, supporting each other's evolving needs, and embracing change as a team—we can turn life's challenges into opportunities for deeper connection and mutual growth. Our commitment to flexibility and open dialogue has allowed us to maintain a harmonious and loving relationship, no matter what life throws our way.

Moreover, embracing the philosophy of "do your best and forget the rest" has taught us to focus on what we can control and to let go of unnecessary stressors. This mindset fosters a compassionate and supportive environment where both partners feel valued and understood, strengthening the foundation of your relationship.

SECTION 3: THE POWER OF INTIMACY AND HAVING A HEART OF SACRIFICE

Let's dive into what truly keeps a relationship alive and thriving: intimacy and the willingness to put your partner's needs alongside your own. Remember those early days when passion and closeness seemed to come so effortlessly? The late-night conversations, the butterflies in your stomach, the feeling that you could conquer anything as long as you were together. As time goes on, it's natural for that initial spark to feel like it's fading a bit. But here's the thing—that doesn't mean your love is any less real or strong. It just means your relationship is evolving, and with that comes the opportunity to deepen your connection in new and meaningful ways.

In this section, we're going to explore practical ways to build and maintain passion in your relationship. This isn't just about physical closeness, though that's certainly a part of it. It's also about nurturing your emotional health and the deeper connection you share as a couple. We'll talk about how to keep the lines of communication open, how to stay engaged in each other's lives, and how to make time for the moments that matter.

We'll look at what it truly means to be there for each other—to support one another emotionally and keep the flame of intimacy burning bright. Life has a way of throwing curveballs, and it's during these times that our relationships can either falter or grow stronger. We'll discuss strategies for staying connected even when things get tough, and how small gestures can make a big difference.

We'll also go into the role of sacrifice in a healthy relationship. Now, I know the word "sacrifice" might sound heavy, but stay with me. Sacrifice doesn't mean losing yourself or constantly putting your needs aside. It's about understanding that sometimes, giving a part of ourselves for the sake of our partner can actually deepen our bond. It's about those moments when you choose to support your partner's dreams, even if it means adjusting your own plans. Or when you offer a listening ear, even if you're tired after a long day.

By understanding these elements and applying some practical strategies, you can keep your relationship vibrant and full of life, no matter how many years you've been together. We'll explore ways to reignite the spark, deepen your emotional connection, and cultivate a heart that's willing to give. So let's get started on this journey together, discovering how intimacy and a spirit of generosity can transform your relationship into something even more beautiful.

CHAPTER 7: PASSIONATE PARTNERS

Passion within a romantic relationship is one of the most vital aspects of a healthy connection. It's the spark that keeps the fire alive, fostering intimacy in nearly every way. Without passion, a relationship can feel dull and lifeless. Passion brings warmth, comfort, excitement, and the acceptance we all desire. It's something that needs to be nurtured and safeguarded to thrive.

But passion isn't just about physical attraction or romance; it's about a deep connection that energizes and sustains your relationship. You can find it in the small, everyday moments just as much as in grand gestures. It's in the way you share a laugh over an inside joke or how a simple touch can convey so much without words. When you feel passionate about your partner, every aspect of your relationship benefits. It encourages you to be more open, vulnerable, and connected.

Maintaining this passion requires continual investment. It means making time for each other, expressing love and appreciation, and keeping the spark alive through shared activities and meaningful conversations. It might involve planning a surprise date night, trying out a new hobby together, or simply setting aside time each day to really talk and listen. Protecting your passion involves setting boundaries, prioritizing your relationship, and being mindful of the factors that can erode intimacy—like neglecting quality time or allowing external stresses to create distance.

When you foster passion, you create a strong foundation that helps you weather the ups and downs of life together.

It's about finding joy in each other's presence and keeping the bond vibrant. Passion is the glue that holds you together, making your relationship not just survive but thrive.

In this chapter, we'll explore practical ways to cultivate and protect passion in your relationship. We'll look at how to keep the flame burning, how to reconnect when you feel the spark fading, and how to safeguard your intimacy against the distractions of everyday life. By understanding and applying these principles, you can keep your relationship vibrant and full of life, no matter how many years you've been together.

ESTABLISHING PASSION

When it comes to building a strong and passionate relationship, setting up a solid foundation is absolutely essential. It's all about open communication and understanding each other's needs and desires right from the start. One key aspect that's sometimes overlooked is discussing physical intimacy—specifically, how often you'd both like to be intimate. It might feel a bit awkward to bring up, but trust me, having this conversation early on can make a world of difference.

I remember when my wife and I first started dating, we had this straightforward talk about what intimacy meant to each of us. We shared our expectations, our comfort levels, and how important that physical connection was in our relationship. It wasn't the easiest conversation, but it brought us so much closer and helped us avoid misunderstandings down the line.

Establishing a mutual understanding about intimacy sets a strong foundation for your relationship. It's not about creating a strict schedule but about knowing what makes each other feel loved and connected. When both partners feel their needs are being met, it builds trust and deepens your emotional bond. Plus, it opens the door to ongoing conversations as your relationship grows and changes.

But laying the foundation isn't just about the physical side. It's also about figuring out how you both express and receive love in general. Maybe you feel most loved when your partner spends quality time with you, while they feel most appreciated through words of affirmation or acts of service. Understanding each other's love languages can make a huge difference. It helps you support each other in ways that really resonate.

Creating routines that foster connection can also strengthen your foundation. It could be a weekly date night, a morning coffee together, or even just sending each other thoughtful messages during the day. These small but consistent gestures show your commitment and keep the connection strong. They're like little reminders that you're both in this together.

Of course, every relationship has its challenges, especially in the beginning. Differences in communication styles or expectations can lead to bumps in the road. But addressing these issues openly and respectfully helps you navigate them as a team. It's important to create a safe space where both of you feel comfortable sharing your thoughts and feelings, no matter how vulnerable they might be.

So, laying the foundation for passion is really about being intentional—having those open conversations about intimacy and expectations, understanding each other's needs, and establishing routines that keep you connected. By doing this, you're setting yourselves up for a passionate and enduring relationship that can grow and adapt over time.

GROWING PASSION

Once you've built that strong foundation, the next step is keeping the passion alive as life evolves. Let's face it—people grow, circumstances shift, and new challenges come up all the time. But here's the thing: you can only fall out of love if you stop nurturing your passion as a couple.

In my own marriage, we've both gone through significant changes—becoming parents, new jobs, different interests, personal growth. Instead of letting these changes create distance, we've made a point to support each other and embrace the new things we bring to the table. It keeps things interesting and helps us continue to connect on a deeper level.

It's so easy to get caught up in routines and let the daily grind take over. Work gets busy, responsibilities pile up, and before you know it, you might feel like you're just coexisting rather than truly connecting. That's why it's so important to make a conscious effort to go above and beyond for each other, even when you're tired or stressed.

Simple gestures can make a big difference. Maybe you surprise your partner with their favorite meal after a long day, or plan a weekend getaway to a place they've always wanted to visit. It doesn't have to be extravagant—the thoughtfulness behind the gesture is what counts. These acts of love remind your partner that they're cherished and that you're willing to invest time and effort into the relationship.

Physical intimacy continues to play a crucial role as well. As life changes, so might your needs and desires. Keep the lines of communication open about how you're feeling and what you need from each other. Sometimes, reconnecting physically can help bridge emotional gaps and bring you closer together. It's not just about the act itself, but about maintaining that intimate connection that strengthens your bond.

Remember to embrace change rather than fear it. See it as an opportunity to learn more about each other and to grow as a couple. Maybe you take up a new hobby together or support each other's individual pursuits. Staying curious about your partner keeps the relationship dynamic and prevents it from becoming stagnant.

Celebrating your journey together is also important. Take time to reflect on the experiences you've shared and the obstacles you've overcome. Maybe you revisit the place where you first met or look through old photos and reminisce. Acknowledging how far you've come reinforces your bond and keeps the passion alive.

At the end of the day, maintaining passion amid life's changes is about continuous effort and intentionality. It's about choosing each other every day, supporting one another through the ups and downs, and never taking your connection for granted. By actively nurturing your relationship—both emotionally and physically—you ensure that your love not only survives but thrives, no matter what life throws your way.

PROTECTING PASSION

Keeping the passion alive in a relationship isn't just about nurturing it—it's also about protecting it. It's important to establish safeguards with and for each other, learning to identify and communicate about things that can potentially harm your intimacy. Sometimes, even things we might not immediately consider, like excessive screen time or something like porn, can create distance between you and your partner without you even realizing it.

Protecting your passion requires taking proactive steps. Think of it as setting up boundaries and agreements that help maintain the health of your relationship. These safeguards act like a shield, keeping your intimacy safe from threats and distractions. They ensure that your relationship stays strong and that both of you remain focused on each other.

It's crucial to be aware of things that can kill your intimacy. Beyond the obvious, there are subtle factors that can creep in—emotional distance, unresolved conflicts, neglecting quality time together, or even getting too caught up in work or hobbies. There's been several times when my wife and I were both so absorbed in either our jobs or our kids that we barely spent any quality time together. It wasn't intentional, but it started to create a gap between us. Recognizing that, we made a conscious effort to set aside time just for us, and it made a huge difference.

Having honest and open conversations about your intimacy can make all the difference. Talk about what you need, what worries you, and how you can support each other in keeping your relationship healthy and passionate. These discussions build trust and understanding. They ensure that both of you are on the same page and committed to protecting what you have together.

For example, you might decide to limit screen time in the evenings so you can focus on each other without distractions. Or perhaps you'll agree to always address conflicts before going to bed, so nothing festers overnight. Being transparent about any struggles or temptations fosters honesty and strengthens your bond.

Remember, protecting your passion is an ongoing journey. It's about being proactive and intentional every day. By setting safeguards and communicating openly, you create a strong defense against anything that might threaten your intimacy. It's not always easy, but investing this effort helps keep your relationship vibrant and fulfilling.

At the end of the day, it's about prioritizing each other and being mindful of the factors that can impact your connection. By doing so, you not only protect the passion you share but also deepen the trust and love between you. It's a commitment to each other that says, "Our relationship matters, and we're willing to do what it takes to keep it strong."

CLOSING SUMMARY

Passion is the heartbeat of a thriving relationship, but it requires consistent care, communication, and intentionality to keep it alive. From establishing a strong foundation to nurturing the flame as life evolves, passion isn't just about grand gestures—it's about the small, everyday moments of connection. Whether it's sharing an inside joke, making time for each other amidst busy schedules, or being open about your needs and desires, passion grows when you're both committed to investing in the relationship.

Protecting your passion is equally important. By setting boundaries, addressing distractions, and having open conversations about intimacy and emotional needs, you create a safe space for your connection to flourish. It's about being mindful of the factors that could weaken your bond and taking proactive steps to keep your relationship strong and vibrant.

At the heart of it, passion isn't something that fades unless it's neglected. By continuing to nurture, grow, and protect your connection, you ensure that your relationship remains full of life, love, and joy—no matter how many years you've been together.

Recommended Reading

"Crazy Good Sex" by Dr. Les Parrott

"Sexperiment" by Ed Young

CHAPTER 8: EMOTIONAL TRUST

How we feel within our marriage affects just about every aspect of our lives. I remember one morning when Lauren and I had a bit of a disagreement before I left for work. It wasn't anything major—just one of those silly arguments—but it stuck with me all day. I found myself distracted during meetings, replaying the conversation in my head, and even my coworkers noticed I was a bit off. It's surprising how a small fight with your spouse can ripple through your entire day, isn't it?

Keeping a pulse on the emotional health of your relationship is so important. When things feel off between Lauren and me, it doesn't just stay at home—it follows us wherever we go. It affects our moods, our productivity, and even how we interact with other people. Recognizing these moments helps us understand what might need to change or improve in how we communicate and connect with each other.

A disagreement or unresolved issue doesn't just stay within the walls of your home. It shadows you throughout your day, coloring your experiences and interactions. You might snap at a coworker without meaning to or find it hard to concentrate on tasks that usually come easily. This ripple effect really highlights how intertwined our emotional well-being and our marriage are.

Trust is the bedrock of any strong relationship. Without it, the essential components of a healthy marriage—like intimacy, love, and open communication—start to crumble. When trust is shaky, you might find yourself feeling disconnected during intimate moments or holding back in conversations, afraid to fully express yourself.

Recognizing when things feel off in your marriage isn't always comfortable, but it's crucial. It's the first step toward healing and growth. By addressing these issues head-on, you can strengthen your relationship and enhance your overall emotional health. After all, a strong emotional connection with your partner not only makes your marriage more fulfilling but also positively impacts every other area of your life.

IMPACT ON SEX

In marriage, emotional trust is the cornerstone that supports every aspect of the relationship, especially intimacy. When you and your partner trust each other emotionally, it creates a safe space where vulnerability and closeness can flourish. However, when emotional trust is compromised, it can create barriers that hinder both emotional and physical connection.

Think about a time when you felt completely emotionally secure with your partner. That sense of trust likely made it easier to open up, share your deepest thoughts, and engage in intimacy without reservations. Emotional trust allows you to be your authentic self, fostering a deeper connection that enhances your relationship on all levels.

On the other hand, when emotional trust is lacking, it can significantly impact your desire for intimacy. Doubts and insecurities might creep in, causing you to hold back or withdraw altogether. For some couples, breaches in emotional trust—whether due to misunderstandings, unfulfilled promises, or emotional neglect—can lead to a decrease in sexual frequency or even a complete pause in their intimate life. This isn't uncommon, and it often signals that deeper issues need to be addressed.

Emotional trust issues can stem from various sources—past hurts, lack of emotional support, or feeling misunderstood. Even small breaches of trust can accumulate over time, creating a significant impact on your relationship. It's essential to recognize these signs early on and address them openly with your partner.

For couples who aren't having regular sex, emotional trust might be both a cause and a symptom of underlying problems. A lack of intimacy can lead to feelings of rejection or emotional distance, further eroding trust. Conversely, existing emotional trust issues might make one or both partners hesitant to engage in physical intimacy, fearing vulnerability or additional hurt.

Rebuilding emotional trust requires patience, honesty, and a willingness to be vulnerable. Open communication is key. Sit down with your partner and share your feelings without assigning blame. Listen actively to their perspective as well. It's about creating a dialogue where both of you feel heard and understood.

Sometimes, professional support can be incredibly helpful. Seeking guidance from a counselor or therapist doesn't mean your relationship is failing; it shows a commitment to making it stronger. They can provide tools and strategies to navigate emotional trust issues and improve your connection.

Remember that rebuilding emotional trust doesn't happen overnight. It takes consistent effort and small, meaningful actions. Showing empathy, being reliable, and expressing appreciation can slowly restore the confidence you have in each other. As emotional trust rebuilds, you'll often find that your desire for intimacy returns as well.

Feeling emotionally secure with your partner allows you to relax and be fully present during intimate moments. It reignites passion and deepens the bond between you. In marriage, intimacy is more than just a physical act; it's an expression of love, trust, and connection.

By prioritizing emotional trust and working through issues together, you create a solid foundation for a fulfilling and passionate relationship. It's a journey that requires effort from both partners, but the rewards—a deeper connection, renewed intimacy, and a stronger bond—are well worth it.

IMPACT ON LOVE

Love is more than just a feeling—it's an action and a choice we make every day. It's something we have to constantly communicate and show to keep our relationships strong and our emotional trust intact. When we trust our partner emotionally, it creates a safe space where love can flourish. But if one of you doesn't feel loved or trusted by the other, you might become emotionally defensive or start to withdraw. You might find yourself taking things the wrong way or shutting down communication altogether. These are signs that your trust in your spouse's love and affection feels insecure and needs a boost.

Rather than waiting for your partner to make the first move, try extending the kind of gesture you'd like to receive. By actively showing love and working to rebuild emotional trust, you can break the cycle of defensiveness and disconnection. Trust isn't just about believing your partner won't hurt you; it's about feeling confident that they care deeply for you and are committed to the relationship.

I recall a time when Lauren and I were both overwhelmed with work, kids and finances. We started to feel distant, and little misunderstandings would quickly escalate into bigger issues. I noticed that I was becoming more defensive, interpreting her words in ways she didn't intend. It became clear that our emotional trust was wavering because we weren't feeling as connected or supported by each other.

Instead of waiting for her to bridge the gap, I decided to take the initiative. I simply walked over to her and hugged her tightly and intimately as I said, "I love you and want you in my life." By choosing to show love and rebuild that emotional trust, we were able to strengthen our bond. It reminded both of us that we're on the same team, and it helped restore the confidence we have in each other's love and commitment.

Emotional trust is the foundation that allows love to be openly expressed and received. When trust is strong, you feel secure in your partner's affection, and you're more likely to interpret their actions positively. However, when trust is lacking, insecurities can lead to misinterpretations and emotional distance. This can create a cycle where both partners feel unloved and unsupported, making it harder to reconnect.

By being proactive in showing love and fostering emotional trust, you create a positive cycle that reinforces your connection. Keep the lines of communication open and be honest about how you're feeling. If you notice your partner seems insecure or withdrawn, offer reassurance and show them affection in meaningful ways. Small, consistent acts of love—like a warm hug, a thoughtful note, or simply asking about their day—can make a significant difference in rebuilding trust.

Remember, love and emotional trust are ongoing choices and efforts. By actively choosing to show love and build trust every day, you reinforce your commitment and strengthen the foundation of your relationship. It's about making your partner feel valued and cherished consistently, not just when everything is going smoothly. By extending gestures of love and nurturing emotional trust, especially during challenging times, you keep your connection strong and your relationship healthy.

It's also important to lead by example. If you're feeling unloved or uncertain about your partner's feelings, take the first step. Showing love can inspire your partner to reciprocate, helping to rebuild emotional trust from both sides. After all, a strong relationship is a partnership where both people actively contribute to the health and happiness of the other.

In the end, maintaining emotional trust and expressing love are intertwined. They feed into each other, creating a resilient bond that can weather the ups and downs of life. By being mindful of this connection and putting in the effort to nurture it, you ensure that your relationship remains a source of joy, support, and deep fulfillment.

IMPACT ON COMMUNICATION

In any romantic relationship, emotional trust is the foundation that holds everything together. In marriage, communication plays a vital role in building and maintaining that trust. Words have the power to strengthen the bond between you and your partner, acting like fans to the flame of passion. Conversely, silence can be a breeding ground for insecurity and doubt. When frustrations and fights occur, it's easy to retreat into silence, but that's often when emotional trust begins to waver.

I recall a time when Lauren and I had a misunderstanding that left both of us feeling hurt. Instead of talking it out, we withdrew from each other, thinking that space would help ease the tension. But in that silence, insecurities started to creep in. I began to wonder if she was still upset or if she didn't want to resolve the issue. She probably felt the same way. It wasn't until we finally sat down and opened up about our feelings that we could rebuild the emotional trust that had been shaken. That conversation reminded me of how crucial open communication is in preserving the trust between us.

Communication is more than just exchanging words; it's about sharing your inner world with your partner. Regular, meaningful conversations help build a strong foundation of emotional trust. When you express your thoughts, feelings, and experiences openly, you invite your partner into your life, deepening your connection. This openness reassures them that you value their presence and are committed to the relationship.

On the other hand, prolonged silence, especially after conflicts, can erode emotional trust. Unspoken feelings and unresolved issues create distance and misunderstanding. Your partner might start to question where they stand with you, leading to feelings of insecurity.

Breaking the silence and addressing issues head-on is essential to prevent these negative feelings from festering.

Making communication a priority is vital for maintaining emotional trust. Simple daily conversations about your day, your emotions, and your thoughts can make a significant difference. It's not always about having deep or serious discussions; sometimes, it's the little chats that keep you connected. Consistent communication shows your partner that you're invested in the relationship and willing to work through challenges together.

After a disagreement, don't let silence define your relationship. It might be uncomfortable, but taking the initiative to start a conversation demonstrates your commitment to resolving conflicts and moving forward. By addressing issues promptly, you prevent small misunderstandings from turning into bigger problems. Open dialogue fosters healing and understanding, strengthening the emotional trust between you.

Creating a safe space where your partner feels comfortable expressing themselves without fear of judgment is also crucial. When both of you can be open and vulnerable, it deepens your emotional connection. Active listening plays a big part in this. Truly hearing what your partner has to say and acknowledging their feelings reinforces trust and shows that you care.

Expressing appreciation and gratitude regularly can bolster emotional trust as well. Let your partner know that you value them and recognize their efforts. Positive communication reinforces love and strengthens your bond.

By prioritizing communication, you're actively nurturing the emotional trust that is so vital to a healthy marriage. Use your words to bridge gaps and prevent insecurity from taking root in silence. When you make an effort to communicate openly and honestly, especially during challenging times, you'll find that your relationship becomes more resilient and fulfilling. Emotional trust isn't built overnight; it's cultivated through consistent, heartfelt communication and a willingness to be present with each other.

CLOSING SUMMARY

Emotional trust is the foundation of a thriving marriage, affecting everything from intimacy to communication. When trust is strong, it creates a safe space where love can flourish, conversations flow freely, and both partners feel secure and valued. However, when emotional trust is compromised, it can cause distance, insecurity, and misunderstandings that ripple through every aspect of the relationship.

Maintaining emotional trust requires ongoing effort, open communication, and a commitment to resolving issues before they grow into larger problems. Whether it's through small gestures of love, actively listening, or addressing intimacy concerns, nurturing emotional trust is essential to keeping the connection strong. Rebuilding trust after it's been shaken takes patience and vulnerability, but the rewards—deeper intimacy, renewed passion, and a stronger bond—are worth the effort.

By prioritizing emotional trust, you create a relationship where both partners feel safe, understood, and loved. It's the bedrock that supports your ability to weather life's challenges and grow together in a meaningful, fulfilling partnership.

Marriage Tip

The next time that you feel disconnected or like you both are repeatedly irritating one another, consider how long it has been since you were physically intimate with one another. Maybe putting all things aside so that you both can connect through sex is exactly what you need.

CHAPTER 9: 100% FOR 100%

The term "50/50" gets tossed around a lot when people talk about relationships, doesn't it? But I've always felt that it's more suited for business deals than for something as intimate and passionate as a marriage. Thinking of a relationship as a 50/50 split gives the impression that it's a conditional contract—I'll do my part if you do yours. But true love and commitment go so much deeper than keeping score or dividing things equally. It's about giving selflessly and trusting that your partner will do the same for you.

In my marriage with Lauren, I've learned what it truly means to sacrifice for someone else, knowing that she's also giving of herself for me. This kind of mutual giving strengthens our bond and deepens our connection. It's not about keeping track of who did what or who owes whom. It's about being there for each other wholeheartedly, especially when life gets tough.

I remember when Lauren was going through a particularly stressful time. She was exhausted, both physically and emotionally. Without a second thought, I took on more of the household responsibilities—not because I expected something in return, but because I wanted to support her in any way I could. Later on, when I faced my own challenges, she was there for me just the same. That's the beauty of giving 100%—it creates a cycle of love and support that keeps the relationship strong.

Putting this idea into practice happens in several ways. Through practical gestures, we show our love in tangible actions—like making each other coffee in the morning or handling chores without being asked. Mentally, it means staying committed and supportive, even during tough times. It's about maintaining a mindset that prioritizes your partner's well-being and the health of your relationship. And then there's forgiveness. Letting go of past hurts and moving forward together is crucial. Forgiveness isn't always easy, but it's a vital part of any loving relationship.

Each of these areas—practical gestures, mental commitment, and forgiveness—offers a unique way to show love and deepen your connection. Embracing these principles helps you move beyond the 50/50 mindset and creates a marriage that is truly fulfilling and resilient. When both partners commit to giving 100%, you build a foundation that can withstand whatever life throws your way.

PRACTICAL GESTURES

In marriage, practical gestures are the heartbeat of daily life—they're the tangible ways we express love and appreciation. These actions often reflect our love languages and are woven into the fabric of our routines. It could be as simple as giving a kiss on the cheek before heading off to work, surprising your partner with a small gift, leaving a heartfelt note, or anything else that's unique to your relationship. The key is to give wholeheartedly, embracing the "100% for 100%" mindset, rather than holding back and waiting for your partner to make the first move.

I remember many mornings when I was rushing to get ready for work, and Lauren would leave a small love note for me to find in my lunch later. It was a small gesture, but it made a difference. Simple moments like these reinforce how selfless practical gestures can strengthen our bond.

Often, couples start to hold back these gestures because they're keeping a mental scoreboard. They hesitate to reach out until they receive what they believe is their remaining 50%. But love isn't about keeping track of who did what; it's about giving freely and trusting that your partner will do the same. When we let go of that scoreboard mentality, we open ourselves up to a more generous and loving relationship.

Understanding and remembering each other's love languages can make these gestures even more meaningful. Everyone has different ways they prefer to give and receive love. By tailoring your actions to what makes your partner feel most loved—whether it's words of affirmation, acts of service, receiving gifts, quality time, or physical touch—you ensure that they feel valued and understood.

Giving without expectation is another essential aspect of practical gestures. It's about focusing on the joy of making your partner happy and strengthening your bond, rather than anticipating something in return. When you give selflessly, you contribute to a positive cycle of generosity and love in your relationship. I find that the more I give freely, the more fulfilled and connected we both feel.

Consistency is also important. Making practical gestures a regular part of your relationship keeps the connection strong and shows your ongoing commitment. It's not about grand displays of affection every time; it's the everyday acts of kindness that truly matter. Simple things like checking in during the day, offering to help with a task, or just listening when your partner needs to talk can make a significant impact.

Expressing appreciation reinforces these positive actions. Let your partner know how much you appreciate their gestures. When Lauren leaves me a note of encouragement before a big presentation or surprises me with my favorite meal, I make sure to tell her how much it means to me. This acknowledgment not only makes her feel valued but also encourages more loving actions from both of us.

By embracing practical gestures and giving 100% of ourselves, we cultivate a relationship that's rich in love and understanding. It's about being there for each other wholeheartedly, without reservations or expectations, and finding joy in the act of giving. When both partners adopt this mindset, the relationship becomes more fulfilling and resilient, capable of weathering any challenges that come your way.

Letting go of the mental scoreboard frees you from unnecessary tension and competition. It allows love to flow more naturally, fostering a supportive and nurturing environment. In the end, it's these selfless acts and the willingness to give your all that strengthen the bond between you and your partner, making your marriage not just a partnership, but a true union of hearts and minds.

MENTALITY

In marriage, mentally letting go of the checklist that keeps tabs on your spouse's efforts is crucial. Love isn't about keeping score or making sure everything is split down the middle. At the end of the day, you should strive to show love to your partner that's not based on conditions or expectations. This becomes especially important when one of you is struggling emotionally or mentally. The contract mentality—the idea that you give only as much as you receive—doesn't account for the hard times we all go through.

Imagine your partner is going through a rough patch and can only give you about 30%. If you're feeling 100%, are you going to hold yourself back because they aren't fulfilling all of your needs at the moment? Many couples fall into this trap, setting themselves up for unnecessary hurt and broken trust. But love isn't always equal in measurable terms, and that's okay.

Throwing out the mental checklist allows you to love more unconditionally and freely. When you stop tallying who did what, you open the door to a deeper, more resilient bond. Focusing on unconditional love means supporting your partner regardless of their current capacity. It's about being there for each other wholeheartedly, not just when everything is perfectly balanced.

The contract mentality fails to account for these inevitable hard times. Expecting equal effort at all times isn't realistic. Life's challenges can affect how much each person can give, and understanding this is crucial for a strong partnership. When you support each other without keeping score, you build a foundation of trust and mutual respect.

It's important to recognize that your partner may not always be able to give 100%. When they're struggling, whether emotionally or mentally, they need your support more than ever. Stepping up when your partner is down not only strengthens your relationship but also shows your commitment to being there through thick and thin.

So how do you put this mentality into practice? Focus on what you can give, not on what you can get. Show love and support without expecting immediate returns. Practice empathy by putting yourself in your partner's shoes—understand their struggles and offer support accordingly. Communicate openly about your needs and be receptive to theirs. Adjust your expectations and recognize that it's okay if one of you is giving more at certain times. By reinforcing trust and showing that you can be relied upon, especially during tough times, you reinforce your commitment to each other.

Embracing this approach moves you beyond the 50/50 mindset and helps create a marriage that's truly fulfilling and resilient. It's about giving 100% of yourself and trusting that your partner is doing the same, even if it doesn't always look equal in the moment. This mindset fosters a deeper connection and builds a relationship that can weather any storm.

FORGIVENESS

Forgiveness is one of those things that's not just essential to marriage—it's essential to any deep relationship. The idea that we're supposed to give 100% of ourselves to each other, instead of the old 50-50 rule, becomes a real challenge when things get tough. But that's when forgiveness comes into play. Jesus didn't just teach us to forgive; He showed us that real love is choosing to love even when the other person doesn't seem to deserve it. That's the heart of forgiveness: choosing to extend grace when it's hardest. And in a relationship, when we choose to forgive, we're saying that the bond between us is worth more than the individual mistakes we've made along the way.

Imagine how many conflicts could be resolved if both people stepped forward, not to prove who was right, but to simply say, "I forgive you." It doesn't mean sweeping issues under the rug—it means allowing space for love to come in, even in the mess of disagreements. Sometimes, forgiveness looks like moving past the need to "win" an argument, and instead, prioritizing peace and connection.

Think about those times when you and your partner are so frustrated that you can barely talk to each other. You sit there in the thick silence, both feeling justified in your hurt. And then, in the midst of that tension, what would happen if your partner just reached out and held you? No words, no justifications, just an embrace. In those moments, something shifts. It's like the walls of pride crumble when met with a simple act of love. That's the power of forgiveness. It doesn't erase the issue, but it shows that the relationship is more important than the issue. It reminds you that the goal is always connection, not being right.

In my own marriage with Lauren, we've learned that the moments where we choose to extend that grace, even when we don't feel like it, are the moments that make us stronger. It's not about who gives more or who deserves more—it's about both of us giving everything. And forgiveness is part of that everything.

The challenge is to not hold onto grudges. The truth is, holding onto old hurts doesn't just affect your partner—it weighs you down too. It's like keeping a running tally of wrongs, and at some point, the weight becomes too much for either of you to carry. But when you let it go, when you really let it go, you make room for something new. You make room for healing. You make room for growth.

Forgiveness isn't a one-time deal either. It's an ongoing practice. There are times when you have to wake up and choose to forgive something from yesterday that's still nagging at you. Or, maybe it's a deeper wound from years ago that still stings. But every time you choose forgiveness, you choose love. And love, especially when it's hard, is what keeps relationships alive.

It doesn't always have to be grand gestures either. Sometimes it's the simple things that reinforce forgiveness and connection—like holding hands after an argument or saying "I love you" when words feel hard to find. It's those moments when we remind ourselves that no matter how intense the conflict, we're still on the same team. We're not fighting against each other—we're fighting for each other.

In the end, forgiveness becomes the foundation of a strong relationship. It's how we move forward without dragging the past into our future. When both people give 100%, and both are committed to letting love lead, it changes everything. There's more peace, more laughter, more understanding. And when conflicts arise, which they inevitably will, you'll both know that love and forgiveness will always bring you back to each other.

CLOSING SUMMARY

A strong, lasting relationship isn't about keeping score; it's about giving 100% of yourself and trusting that your partner will do the same. When we move beyond the "50/50" mindset, we open ourselves to a deeper connection built on selflessness, love, and mutual support. Practical gestures, like simple acts of kindness, and a mentality that embraces unconditional love, create a positive cycle that strengthens the relationship. Forgiveness is the glue that holds everything together, allowing us to move past hurt and build something even stronger.

By giving fully, without expectations, you and your partner create a foundation that can withstand challenges. It's not about always being perfectly balanced; it's about being there for each other, even when life feels uneven. Love, trust, and forgiveness keep the relationship growing and thriving, making your partnership more fulfilling and resilient.

SECTION 4: COMPATIBILITY AND COMMITMENT

This section is all about understanding what it really means to be committed to each other, not just in words but in action and emotional connection. The truth is, compatibility isn't something you either have or don't—it's something that evolves over time as you grow and change. The goal here is to help you see how important it is to not only communicate your emotions openly but to do it in a way that strengthens your relationship, rather than creating more tension.

We'll get into what it looks like to handle disagreements without letting them tear you apart. Conflict is inevitable, but how you handle it is what determines whether it builds a wall between you or brings you closer. When you learn to share your feelings in a way that invites understanding rather than defense, you can work through the hardest moments together. It's about finding the right balance between expressing your needs and being willing to listen to theirs.

Life changes all of us, and those changes can sometimes shake the foundation of a relationship if you're not careful. Maybe you or your partner goes through a career shift, personal growth, or just a different way of seeing the world. These shifts can challenge your compatibility if you don't learn to adapt together. This section will show you how to navigate those changes and remain connected through it all. It's not about staying the same, but about growing together, finding new ways to stay compatible, and supporting each other through life's inevitable ups and downs.

When we talk about commitment, it's not just about staying in the same house or wearing a ring. True commitment shows up in the everyday moments—the way you choose to support each other, even when it's inconvenient or difficult. It's the emotional and physical presence you offer, the way you prioritize each other, and the way you keep showing up no matter what. It's in the small acts of love, and in the bigger decisions that demonstrate you're in it for the long haul.

As you go through this section, you'll gain more insight into how to build a relationship that's not just about surviving but thriving. You'll see how to address differences with care, embrace the changes that come, and embody a commitment that creates a relationship built on trust, love, and mutual respect. The goal is for your relationship to be one that not only endures but also deepens with time, becoming more resilient and connected as you continue to grow together.

CHAPTER 10: EMOTIONAL TRANSPARENCY

Emotional transparency is one of the most powerful tools for deepening a relationship, but it's also one of the trickiest things to master. Emotions can be so simple and straightforward—you're angry, and you know exactly why. But other times, they can feel overwhelming or confusing, and you can't quite put your finger on what's bothering you. That's perfectly normal. We all experience moments where our emotions feel clear and other times where they seem like a tangled web. The key is learning how to communicate those feelings, whether they make perfect sense to you or not.

Expressing your emotions clearly isn't something that comes naturally to everyone—it's an art form that takes practice. Sometimes it's not just about identifying what you're feeling, but finding the right words to share it in a way that helps your partner understand. When you get in the habit of communicating openly about your feelings, you'll not only understand yourself better but also allow your partner to support you in ways that actually matter.

But communication is a two-way street, and listening is just as important as speaking. When your partner opens up about their feelings, it's about creating a space where they feel truly heard and understood. Being a good listener means offering more than just advice—it means making your partner feel safe enough to share their emotions without fear of judgment. That sense of safety and understanding is what strengthens your bond and builds trust, and over time, it becomes the foundation that makes your relationship more resilient.

Emotional transparency isn't just about knowing how to talk to each other; it's about learning how to navigate each other's emotional worlds. It's not always easy, but it's worth the effort. As both of you practice sharing and listening, you'll find that the ups and downs of life feel less overwhelming because you're handling them together. You'll develop a deeper, more empathetic connection where both of your feelings are respected and taken seriously.

By committing to ongoing emotional transparency, you create a relationship that's more than just functional—it's supportive, loving, and capable of weathering the storms. When both of you feel safe to express yourselves and confident that the other person will listen, you build a relationship where both love and trust can truly flourish.

UNDERSTANDING EMOTIONS

Understanding emotions, especially in a relationship, is like having a map to navigate through tough moments. Before you can explain to your partner what you're feeling, it's important to first understand it yourself. It's easy to feel angry or upset, but often those emotions are just the surface. The real power comes when you take a step back and reflect on what's actually causing them. Maybe it's frustration from work, feeling unappreciated, or an unresolved issue from the past. When you take the time to understand where your feelings are coming from, you're not just reacting—you're responding. And that response is always more productive and less likely to lead to misunderstandings.

In a relationship, especially one where emotions run deep, understanding why you're upset helps you communicate in a way that doesn't add fuel to the fire. The clearer you are with yourself, the clearer you can be with your partner. It's like what they say—knowing why you're mad helps you avoid "talking mad." When you're aware of what's really bothering you, it's easier to express that without it turning into a blow-up. And this doesn't just make things smoother for the moment—it builds a foundation of trust where both people feel safe sharing what's on their minds.

When we're able to articulate our emotions with clarity, it gives our partner the opportunity to understand us better and respond with empathy. Instead of reacting to the surface-level anger or sadness, they can connect with the underlying need or concern. This can prevent those arguments that go in circles because neither of you is really talking about what's going on underneath. Clarity is key to avoiding escalation and creating a space where both of you feel heard, not attacked.

Think about those times when a conversation spirals out of control. Often, it's because neither person fully understands their own emotions before bringing them to the table. That's why taking a moment to understand your feelings before expressing them is crucial. You can still be upset, but you can communicate it in a way that invites dialogue instead of defensiveness. When you know why you're mad, you can talk about it calmly and productively, which almost always leads to a more meaningful resolution.

It's not just about avoiding arguments—it's about creating a deeper connection through honest communication. Taking time for that self-check before approaching your partner allows you to be more mindful in how you speak. And the words you choose matter. Using "I" statements, for instance, shifts the focus from blame to sharing how you feel, which naturally makes the conversation less accusatory and more about solving the issue together.

Sometimes, when emotions are running high, it's easy to let them take control of the conversation. But learning to pause and gather your thoughts before diving into a discussion can make all the difference. It's like a reset button that allows you to approach things with a level head. And this doesn't mean hiding your emotions or waiting until you're perfectly calm—sometimes that pause is just what you need to find the right words instead of letting the anger speak for you.

At the heart of emotional transparency is honesty—first with yourself and then with your partner. If you're not honest about what's really bothering you, how can your partner truly understand? Honesty invites understanding, and when both of you are committed to being open about your feelings, it creates a trust that deepens your bond. Your partner isn't left guessing or trying to read between the lines. They know exactly where you're coming from, and that allows them to meet you where you are emotionally.

Finally, it's just as important to encourage your partner to express their emotions too. Emotional transparency isn't one-sided. It's a practice that both people have to commit to. When both of you feel comfortable sharing your emotions and taking the time to really understand each other, the connection becomes stronger. It's like building a muscle—the more you practice it, the more natural it becomes. And that mutual understanding is what helps you weather the inevitable emotional ups and downs of life together.

COMMUNICATING EMOTIONS

When emotions are running high, staying reasonable and rational can feel like a distant goal. In any relationship, especially romantic ones, it's easy to let your feelings take the lead and speak for you. But when you're emotional, it's important to remember that your feelings—while valid—aren't always the best measure of what's right or wrong. Emotions can cloud judgment and make things seem more black-and-white than they really are. The goal of sharing how you feel should never be about proving who's right or assigning blame; it's about creating a better understanding between you and your partner.

We've all been in those moments where emotions take over, and it feels like the only thing that matters is being heard. But when we give emotions too much control, the conversation can quickly spiral into miscommunication and unresolved conflict. Finding a balance between emotion and reason is key. It's not about shutting down how you feel, but about recognizing that emotions can sometimes distort reality. By approaching your feelings with both heart and mind, you create space for a more constructive and meaningful dialogue.

One of the hardest parts about communicating emotions in any relationship is learning to separate feelings from facts. Feelings are personal—they're your truth in the moment—but that doesn't mean they're the full picture. For instance, you might feel hurt or frustrated, but that feeling may be based on assumptions or misunderstandings. When you start a conversation by acknowledging that your emotions are just one side of the situation, it opens up room for empathy and understanding. This is where real growth happens. You begin to see the situation from a broader perspective, where both your experience and your partner's matter equally.

In a relationship, the aim of sharing your emotions isn't to win or to convince your partner that they're wrong. Instead, it's about building bridges of understanding between the two of you. When you express how you feel with the intent of connecting, you invite your partner into your experience, allowing them to see things through your eyes. This helps create a space where both of you feel heard and respected, rather than defensive or misunderstood.

Communication in these moments requires thoughtfulness. Before diving into a difficult conversation, taking a moment to pause and reflect can make all the difference. A little bit of space helps you get clarity on what you really need to say, and it prevents emotions from hijacking the conversation. When you take that pause, it's easier to approach your partner calmly, even if the topic is sensitive. Staying calm doesn't mean suppressing your feelings; it just means you're making sure those feelings are shared in a way that leads to resolution, not further conflict.

Language plays a huge role in how emotions are communicated. It's tempting to assign blame when you're upset, but words like "You always" or "You never" often make things worse. Shifting the language to focus on your own experience—"I feel hurt when..." or "I'm upset because..."—keeps the conversation focused on building understanding rather than creating distance. This kind of language invites your partner into the discussion instead of pushing them away.

At the same time, communication is a two-way street. Just as important as expressing your feelings is giving your partner the space to share theirs. Active listening, where you're not just waiting for your turn to speak but really hearing what your partner is saying, creates a safe and open dialogue. In those moments, you're not just responding to their words; you're acknowledging their perspective and making them feel valued. That's the foundation of emotional transparency—both partners feeling safe enough to share, and both being heard.

When it comes to resolving conflicts, approaching it as a team is crucial. You're not adversaries trying to defeat each other in an argument. You're two people who care about each other, working together to find a solution that works for both of you. By keeping the focus on solutions instead of dwelling on the problem, you turn a potential point of conflict into an opportunity for growth. It's not always easy, but when both of you commit to understanding each other and addressing each other's needs, you lay the groundwork for a healthier, more connected relationship.

LISTENING AND EMPATHY

Listening and empathy are the cornerstones of emotional transparency in any relationship, but they're especially crucial in romantic ones. It's not enough just to speak your truth—you also have to make space for your partner's truth. Just as much as you want to feel heard and understood, your partner needs that same assurance. But here's the catch: when emotions are high, it's easy to get defensive, especially if what your partner is saying touches on something sensitive. And once defensiveness creeps in, the entire conversation shifts from connection to conflict.

That's why mastering the art of listening and showing empathy is essential for keeping emotional transparency alive.

Listening isn't just about hearing the words your partner says; it's about truly understanding where they're coming from. It's about making them feel valued, like what they're expressing matters to you. Think about it—when you're sharing something vulnerable, don't you feel closer to the person who actually leans in, makes eye contact, and engages with what you're saying? That's the power of active listening. It's not just hearing words; it's being fully present in the moment with your partner. When you do this, you're telling them, "I see you. I hear you. What you're feeling matters to me."

Showing empathy goes hand-in-hand with listening. It's not just about understanding their words; it's about understanding their feelings. Empathy is the ability to put yourself in your partner's shoes and really feel what they're going through. This is where a deeper emotional connection is built. When you can genuinely empathize with your partner, you're showing them that their emotions are valid, that you're with them in whatever they're feeling. And that kind of connection goes far beyond just solving problems—it creates a bond where both of you feel safe and supported.

But let's be real—when someone's sharing their emotions with you, especially if it's about something you did or didn't do, it's easy to feel defensive. It's human nature to want to protect ourselves from feeling wrong or misunderstood. The challenge is to not let that defensiveness take over. When you feel that urge to defend yourself rising up, it's important to pause and remind yourself that this isn't about winning an argument or proving a point. The goal is to understand, not to react. Staying calm and open in these moments allows for real conversation and stops things from escalating into unnecessary conflict.

One of the most helpful strategies in this process is reflecting back what your partner has said. It might sound simple, but paraphrasing their words can work wonders. It lets your partner know you're truly listening, and it also helps avoid misunderstandings. For example, if they say, "I felt hurt when you didn't check in on me after my tough day," reflecting back might sound like, "So what I'm hearing is you needed more support from me after your hard day?" That small act of clarification goes a long way in ensuring that both of you are on the same page. It's about checking in to make sure you really understand before diving into a response.

Another crucial piece is validation. Validating your partner's feelings doesn't mean you have to agree with everything they're saying, but it does mean you acknowledge that their feelings are real and important. Telling your partner, "I understand why you feel this way, and it makes sense," creates a space where they feel safe to continue sharing without fear of being dismissed. And once both of you feel understood, solutions and resolutions naturally become easier to find.

And let's not forget how important it is to stay calm. If you feel that defensiveness creeping in, it's okay to take a beat. Deep breaths can do wonders for resetting your mindset. Remind yourself that the goal isn't to get defensive or prove a point—it's to understand your partner and find a way to move forward together. When both people stay calm, it allows for a much more constructive conversation, even when the topic is tough.

When it's your turn to respond, do so with empathy. Remember, your partner just took the time to share something vulnerable with you, so this is your opportunity to show them you care. Respond with "I" statements, focusing on your own experience without blaming or accusing. For instance, instead of saying, "You never listen to me," try saying, "I feel frustrated when I don't feel heard." This shift in language keeps the conversation focused on understanding and resolution, rather than putting your partner on the defensive.

At the heart of all of this is mutual understanding. When both of you commit to actively listening, showing empathy, and avoiding defensiveness, you're creating a relationship where both people feel safe to share. You're fostering an environment where emotions can be expressed freely and without fear of judgment. And that's where true connection happens. It's not about getting everything right all the time; it's about both of you being willing to show up for each other, even when emotions are tough to navigate.

By practicing these strategies, you'll find that conversations that used to feel overwhelming or frustrating now bring you closer together. You'll both feel more heard, understood, and valued, and in the process, your relationship will grow stronger and more resilient.

CLOSING SUMMARY

Emotional transparency is the heartbeat of a deeply connected and resilient relationship. By openly sharing your feelings and truly listening to your partner, you create a space where both of you feel understood, valued, and supported. Throughout this chapter, we've explored how understanding your emotions, effectively communicating them, and practicing active listening and empathy are essential for building and maintaining emotional transparency.

When you and Lauren commit to being emotionally transparent, you strengthen the foundation of your marriage. This openness not only fosters trust and intimacy but also equips you both to navigate life's challenges together with greater ease and unity. Emotional transparency isn't always easy—it requires patience, vulnerability, and consistent effort—but the rewards are immense. It leads to a more harmonious and fulfilling partnership where both partners feel safe to express themselves and grow together.

Remember, emotional transparency is an ongoing journey. It evolves as your relationship grows and as you both continue to learn more about each other. By prioritizing honest communication and empathetic listening, you ensure that your relationship remains strong and adaptable, capable of weathering any storm that comes your way. Embrace the practice of emotional transparency, and watch as it transforms your marriage into a true partnership of hearts and minds.

Marriage Tip

As a couple, you are co-stars in your shared life story. Both partners are equally valuable and deserve to be heard and understood. The goal of emotional discussions should always be reconciliation and deepened love.

CHAPTER 11: COMPATIBILITY CHANGES

Change is one of the few constants in life, and just like everything else in the world, we as individuals evolve over time. When you're in a long-term relationship, you don't just get to witness these changes in your partner—you're actively part of their journey. As you and your partner go through different seasons of life, you'll both change in ways that may surprise you. How you react to those changes can either bring you closer or drive a wedge between you.

It's important to recognize that the person you fell in love with might not stay the same forever, and that's perfectly natural. Life experiences, challenges, and personal growth shape us into different versions of ourselves over time. Your compatibility as a couple isn't something set in stone—it's fluid and needs to evolve along with the two of you. The key isn't to resist these changes by trying to keep your partner exactly as they were, but to embrace their growth and honor their evolution as part of the relationship's journey.

This is why adaptability is essential in any relationship. Instead of trying to control your partner's growth or wishing they'd stay the same, supporting their evolution is what builds a strong foundation for lasting connection. You don't want to be the person who holds them back; you want to be the one who grows alongside them, encouraging them to become the best version of themselves. That's how relationships deepen over time—by not just tolerating change, but by actively fostering an environment where both people feel free to evolve.

In this chapter, we'll explore how embracing each other's growth, staying open to change, and nurturing adaptability can strengthen your relationship. It's about understanding that change doesn't mean losing what you had—it means gaining something new together. By learning to grow with one another, you'll find that your connection becomes not only more resilient, but also richer and more fulfilling as time goes on.

CHANGE OF INTERESTS

As people grow and evolve, their interests and hobbies often shift. What once sparked excitement in the early stages of your relationship may no longer have the same appeal, and that's perfectly normal. But when these changes happen, they can sometimes create distance if they aren't approached with understanding. The key to navigating these shifts lies in embracing and supporting each other's evolving interests, even when they're different from your own. These changes don't have to be a source of disconnect—in fact, they can be an opportunity to strengthen your bond.

As time goes on, you may find that what excites your partner today is entirely different from what first drew them in years ago. Maybe they used to be passionate about sports, and now they're more interested in painting or photography. These evolving interests affect how you spend time together and the activities you both enjoy. Acknowledging that change is natural, rather than resisting it, allows you both to adapt and maintain a deeper connection. It's about being open to the idea that who your partner is becoming doesn't threaten your relationship—it enriches it.

One of the most meaningful ways to support your partner through these changes is to embrace their new interests. Show genuine curiosity about what lights them up now, even if it's something you don't quite understand or share the same enthusiasm for. This kind of open-mindedness fosters a sense of mutual respect. Your partner feels valued and understood when you take the time to appreciate their passions, even if they've shifted in ways you didn't expect.

But it's not just about accepting each other's interests from a distance—sharing and exploring those new hobbies together can add a fresh sense of excitement to your relationship. When you're both willing to try new things, it keeps the relationship dynamic and engaging. You might discover that you enjoy something you'd never considered before, or at the very least, you'll create new shared experiences that bring you closer. It's about staying open to growth as individuals while still finding ways to grow together.

At the same time, it's crucial to maintain a healthy respect for each other's individuality. While it's wonderful to share interests, it's equally important to give each other space to pursue passions independently. Not every hobby needs to be a joint activity, and that's okay. Encouraging your partner to pursue their own interests without feeling pressured to always do things together creates a balance. This personal space for growth doesn't weaken the relationship—it strengthens it by ensuring that both partners have the freedom to explore who they are while staying connected as a couple.

Navigating these changes is about finding a balance between sharing in each other's growth and maintaining the individuality that keeps the relationship healthy. Having regular check-ins about what's currently exciting you and listening to your partner's evolving passions can make all the difference. It opens up space for conversation, understanding, and collaboration in how you spend your time together.

Being supportive doesn't always mean participating in every new hobby, but it does mean showing an interest in what matters to your partner. Whether it's attending an event they care about or simply listening to them talk about their new passion, that support speaks volumes. And when you find the opportunity to explore new things together—whether it's trying a new sport, learning a new skill, or even just sharing a new show or book—it keeps your relationship lively and connected.

It's also important to remember that it's perfectly okay to have different interests. In fact, those differences are part of what makes your relationship unique. Respecting and encouraging each other's individuality while finding ways to create shared goals is a great way to integrate your evolving interests. Maybe one of you loves photography and the other is passionate about hiking—why not plan a trip together where both of those interests are honored? Finding ways to bridge your individual passions into joint experiences can strengthen your bond and make life more exciting.

At the heart of it all is a willingness to adapt and grow alongside each other. Change doesn't have to be a threat to compatibility—it can be the very thing that keeps your relationship fresh and resilient. By embracing the changes in interests and hobbies, and supporting each other's growth, you're building a relationship that evolves over time, becoming richer and more fulfilling as you both continue to grow into new versions of yourselves.

WORLDVIEW CHANGES

As you journey through life together, your worldview naturally evolves, shaping how you see and treat others. This evolution is a normal part of personal growth, as experiences, challenges, and new insights influence the way you view the world. Whether it's your approach to relationships, social values, or how you engage with friends and family, these changes can significantly impact your marriage. Navigating these shifts with openness and support is essential for maintaining a healthy relationship. The key is recognizing that as you and your partner's perspectives grow and change, your connection can grow stronger too, as long as you embrace these changes with mutual respect and understanding.

When your worldview shifts, it often affects how you relate to others. Maybe the way you once interacted with family members feels different now, or perhaps your views on certain societal issues have shifted over time. These evolving perspectives can alter the dynamics of your relationships with those outside your marriage, which in turn can affect the relationship you have with each other. It's important to navigate these changes together, discussing how your values or beliefs might be influencing how you approach friendships, family ties, and even community involvement.

One of the most meaningful things you can do for each other in this context is to embrace the new perspectives your partner develops. Personal growth isn't always linear, and as your partner evolves, they may start seeing the world in ways they didn't before. Rather than feeling threatened by these shifts, show curiosity and respect for their changing views. Ask questions, engage with their new perspectives, and understand where they're coming from. This open-mindedness strengthens the relationship by fostering mutual respect and deepening your connection. When your partner feels that their personal growth is valued, it reinforces the trust and support that keeps your relationship thriving.

Supporting each other through these changes is crucial. As your partner's worldview shifts, it may affect how they relate to close friends or family members, and those shifts can be complicated to navigate. Open conversations about these evolving perspectives help both of you stay connected. Maybe your partner feels differently now about certain social or political issues, or perhaps they've changed how they view the dynamics within their family. These shifts don't have to create distance between you—Instead, they can be opportunities for shared growth if you approach them with empathy and understanding.

Balancing individual values with shared values can sometimes feel tricky, but it's essential for maintaining harmony in your relationship. While it's great when you share similar perspectives, it's equally important to respect each other's individual views, even when they differ. Encourage open discussions about how your perspectives are changing, and listen without judgment. This approach creates a healthy dynamic where both partners feel heard and respected in their beliefs, rather than feeling pressured to conform to one another. It's about finding the balance between honoring who you are as individuals and nurturing the shared values that bind you together.

Regular conversations about how your views are evolving can keep you connected and prevent misunderstandings from growing into larger issues. Checking in with each other about how you're seeing the world—whether that's in relation to family dynamics, friendships, or societal issues—keeps the lines of communication open. Even if your views don't always align, knowing that you have a safe space to express and explore these perspectives helps both of you feel understood and supported.

Empathy is also key when it comes to navigating these changes. Just as you want your partner to understand and respect your views, it's important to offer the same in return. When your partner shares how their perspective on something has shifted, practice empathy by putting yourself in their shoes and considering their experiences. This helps build a deeper emotional connection and creates an environment where both of you can grow without fear of judgment.

As your worldviews evolve, it's important to maintain strong connections with the people who matter most to you, even as your perspectives change. Adapting your interactions with friends and family to reflect your new values doesn't mean cutting people out—it means engaging with them in ways that feel authentic to who you are now. Supporting each other as you both adjust to these shifts helps keep your important relationships intact while honoring the growth you're experiencing as individuals.

At the same time, remember that it's okay to have different perspectives from each other. What matters most is the mutual respect and willingness to find common ground. Sometimes, you may not agree on everything, and that's perfectly normal. What's important is that you approach these differences with openness, respect, and a desire to understand each other's viewpoints.

Shared activities that reflect both of your values and interests can also help reinforce the common ground in your relationship. Whether it's volunteering together, attending events that align with your values, or simply having meaningful discussions, these shared experiences can strengthen your bond and reaffirm the values that you both hold dear.

Ultimately, by navigating changes in worldview with empathy, support, and open communication, you can create a relationship that adapts and grows with you both. As you embrace each other's evolving perspectives, you'll find that your connection becomes more dynamic, resilient, and understanding. Instead of these changes creating distance, they become opportunities for deeper connection and shared growth, making your relationship stronger as you continue to grow together.

CHANGES IN HOW YOU LIVE AND LOVE

Over time, the ways you live and love naturally change. Life's demands, fluctuating energy levels, and the way you express or receive love are all part of the evolving landscape of a relationship. What worked for you and your partner at the beginning may not be the same things that work for you now. But this is a natural part of growing together, and the key is learning how to communicate openly about these changes and adjusting with empathy and flexibility. When you're both willing to adapt to each other's evolving needs, it keeps your connection strong, even when the way you show love looks different than before.

Navigating changes in energy levels can be one of the biggest challenges in a long-term relationship. Whether it's the result of work stress, health issues, parenting, or just the general ups and downs of life, you and your partner won't always have the same energy to devote to each other. That's okay. The important thing is to recognize that energy levels fluctuate and that this isn't a reflection of how much you care for one another. When you're both aware of these shifts, you can offer the right kind of support at the right time, ensuring that neither of you feels neglected during the more demanding periods of life.

When energy is low, it's easy to misinterpret that lack of energy as a lack of love or effort. But adapting to these shifts is key to maintaining a strong connection. Maybe you're in a phase where grand gestures of affection feel like too much, but a kind word or a quiet moment of connection can mean just as much. Being flexible in how you express love ensures that both partners feel valued, no matter what's going on externally. It's about recognizing that love doesn't have to be loud or extravagant to be meaningful—it just has to be present, even in the smallest ways.

As you grow together, you may also find that the ways you give and receive love evolve. Maybe early in the relationship, acts of service made you feel most loved, but now you find that quality time or words of affirmation hold more weight. This shift is natural, and the key to keeping your bond strong is being aware of these changes. When you recognize that your partner's love language has shifted or your own needs have evolved, you can adjust how you express your affection, ensuring that both of you continue to feel cherished and understood.

Supporting each other through these changes is one of the most important ways to keep the relationship grounded. Life can be exhausting, and there will be times when your partner may need more rest or when they don't have the energy for social activities or big plans. By being aware of their energy levels and showing understanding when they need to take a step back, you create a dynamic where both of you feel supported, even during the low-energy phases. It's about being patient and empathetic, recognizing that love can still thrive in the quieter, more restful moments of life.

Balancing these changes in energy with how you love each other requires open and honest communication. Checking in with each other regularly about how you're feeling, both physically and emotionally, can help prevent misunderstandings. Maybe your partner is going through a particularly stressful time and doesn't have the energy for date nights or long conversations. Instead of feeling disconnected, those regular check-ins allow you to recalibrate how you show love in ways that work for where both of you are at the moment. Even a simple acknowledgment like, "I know things are overwhelming right now, but I'm here for you," can make all the difference.

Being flexible in how you express love is crucial during these times. Just because you don't have the energy for grand gestures doesn't mean love isn't there. A gentle touch, a warm hug, or a kind word can often carry as much weight as more elaborate expressions of affection. By adapting your love language to match your current energy levels, you ensure that love remains a constant presence, even when life feels demanding.

It's also essential to prioritize self-care. Maintaining your own energy levels by getting enough rest, exercise, and relaxation allows you to show up fully in your relationship. You can't pour from an empty cup, so taking care of yourself means you're better able to support your partner when they need you most. And when you both prioritize self-care, it creates a foundation of mutual respect for each other's well-being, which only strengthens your bond.

Understanding your partner's energy levels and being aware of how they give and receive love at different times fosters empathy and connection. When they're going through a low-energy phase, your patience and understanding will speak volumes. When you're the one feeling drained, their flexibility and support will remind you that love doesn't depend on constant activity or outward expression—it's a steady presence, adaptable and resilient.

In the end, adapting to these changes ensures that both of you feel loved and supported, no matter what's going on in life. When you're both willing to navigate the shifts in energy and affection with open communication, you create a relationship that's not only more understanding but also more resilient. By recognizing and honoring each other's evolving needs, you strengthen your connection, ensuring that love remains a source of support, no matter what challenges life throws your way.

CLOSING SUMMARY

Change is just a part of life, and in a long-term relationship, embracing those changes together is what really builds a strong and lasting bond. In this chapter, we talked about how both you and your partner grow and evolve over time.

Instead of trying to hold onto who you were when you first fell in love, supporting each other's journeys helps keep your relationship fresh and dynamic. It's all about growing together rather than growing apart.

We looked at how shifting interests, changing worldviews, and evolving ways of expressing love can sometimes feel like they create distance. But when you embrace each other's new passions and perspectives, it actually enriches your shared experiences. Whether it's taking up a new hobby together, having open conversations about your changing beliefs, or adjusting how you show love to fit your current needs, these adaptations ensure that both of you feel valued and supported, even when life gets hectic.

At the end of the day, compatibility isn't something you achieve once and forget about—it's an ongoing journey that requires flexibility, open communication, and mutual respect. By staying committed to understanding each other's growth and maintaining a supportive environment, you and your partner can navigate the ups and downs with grace and unity. This ability to adapt not only strengthens your bond but also makes your relationship more fulfilling and resilient, turning every change into an opportunity for deeper connection and lasting love.

Marriage Tip:

While you can appreciate the past, you are married to the present. Rather than trying to force your spouse to be the person they used to be, embrace the person who your spouse has become.

CHAPTER 12: COMMITMENT

Commitment in a relationship is more than just a promise or a vow—it's an ongoing choice that we make every day. Love, at its core, is an action and a choice. Those feelings of excitement or the warmth of affection are wonderful, but they're often a response to how we treat one another, not just something that happens automatically. When people say they've "fallen out of love," it's often not because the love disappeared, but because the intentional acts of nurturing that love faded away. It's easy to let the demands of life push a relationship to the back burner, but real love is about choosing each other daily, especially when it's hard.

True commitment in a relationship is meant to withstand the highs and lows. It's easy to love each other when things are going well, but the real strength of your bond shows during the tough moments. Whether it's challenges at work, health issues, or simply the stress of everyday life, your commitment is what carries you through. It's a constant, a foundation that you can lean on when everything else feels uncertain. When the initial sparks fade, what you're left with is the raw, unwavering commitment to one another, and that's the bedrock of a lasting relationship.

Love isn't a one-time decision—it's a continuous effort. It's about making your partner feel valued and appreciated in the little, everyday moments. The small gestures—a kind word, a thoughtful act, or just showing up when it matters—are what keep your connection strong. During the difficult times, it's this choice to stay committed that makes all the difference. When life throws challenges your way, whether financial struggles, health issues, or personal hardships, standing by each other and working through it together only deepens your bond.

At the end of the day, the strength of your relationship is built on these daily choices. Commitment is about more than just staying; it's about actively choosing to invest in your partner and your relationship every single day. It's about choosing to love, even when it's not easy, and holding onto that choice through every season of life. When everything else fades away, that daily decision to love and stand by each other is what sustains a relationship and keeps it thriving.

UNDERSTANDING COMMITMENT

Commitment in marriage isn't something that just happens—it's a conscious choice, one that has to be decided, communicated, and reaffirmed regularly. It's about more than just saying "I'm committed" on your wedding day; it's about making the decision every day to prioritize your relationship, to be present, and to work through challenges together. Before you even say "I do," it's essential that both of you have honest, open conversations about what commitment means to each of you. This means talking about your values, your expectations, and your shared goals. When you're both clear about what commitment looks like, it creates a foundation that's strong enough to weather the ups and downs of life.

One of the biggest misunderstandings about commitment is the assumption that it's automatic. It's not. Both partners have to actively choose to be fully invested, not just when things are easy, but especially when they're hard.

That choice—to be all in, no matter what—sets the tone for your marriage. It's a mutual decision to stick together through thick and thin, even when the road gets bumpy.

Having these conversations early on is crucial. You don't want to leave room for assumptions or misunderstandings when it comes to something as important as your commitment to each other. Talk openly about what you both expect from your relationship, how you plan to navigate challenges, and what your long-term vision for your marriage looks like. This level of transparency sets the stage for a deeper understanding and ensures that you're both on the same page.

Commitment isn't just about staying together—it's about creating a safe space where both of you feel secure and understood. When you know your partner is fully committed to you, it builds trust. It allows you to be vulnerable and open, knowing that your partner is in it for the long haul. This sense of security strengthens the bond between you, creating a relationship where both of you can grow and thrive together. And when life inevitably throws challenges your way, that commitment becomes the anchor that holds you steady, knowing that you're not facing those challenges alone.

But commitment isn't something that you talk about once and then never revisit. It needs to be communicated regularly, both in words and actions. Don't assume your partner knows you're committed just because you said it once. Make it a regular part of your relationship to talk about your dedication to one another. Discuss what commitment looks like in your day-to-day life. Talk about how you'll handle conflicts, how you'll support each other's individual goals, and how you'll prioritize your relationship, even when life gets hectic.

There's immense value in continually reaffirming your commitment. It keeps the relationship grounded and helps both partners feel seen and valued. It's not just about grand gestures—it's about the small, everyday actions that show you're in this together. Whether it's checking in on how each other's day went, planning time for each other despite busy schedules, or simply expressing appreciation for one another, these little things add up. They remind both of you that the relationship is a priority, that you're both committed to making it work.

A powerful way to strengthen your commitment is to create a shared vision for your marriage. Sit down together and talk about what kind of relationship you want to build. What values are important to both of you? What are your goals for the future, both individually and as a couple? Creating this shared vision gives you both a clear understanding of what you're working toward and ensures that you're aligned in your goals and priorities.

Regular check-ins are another way to keep the lines of communication open and ensure that your commitment stays strong. These conversations don't have to be formal, but they should be intentional. Use this time to talk about how you're both feeling about the relationship, what's going well, and where there might be room for improvement. These check-ins provide an opportunity to reaffirm your commitment to one another and address any concerns before they grow into bigger issues.

Commitment is also about investing in each other. It's not enough to simply say you're committed—you have to show it through your actions. This might look like making time for date nights, setting aside time for quality conversations, or supporting each other during tough times. The effort you put into the relationship is what keeps it alive and thriving.

Ultimately, commitment in marriage is about creating a foundation of trust, security, and mutual respect. It's about making sure that both of you feel supported, valued, and loved, not just in the good times but in every moment. By deciding on and clearly communicating your commitment from the beginning—and continuing to nurture it throughout your relationship—you're laying the groundwork for a strong, enduring marriage that can weather any storm. It's not about perfection, but about the daily choices that keep you moving forward together, building a life of love and partnership.

DEMONSTRATING COMMITMENT

Demonstrating commitment In a marriage isn't just about the big gestures or grand declarations—it's about showing up consistently, especially when things aren't going smoothly. True commitment reveals itself not just in the joyful moments, but in the way you stand by each other during life's tougher seasons. It's easy to express your love and dedication when things are going well, but it's in those challenging moments that commitment really proves its depth. When you demonstrate your commitment during hard times, you're letting your partner know that you're in this together, no matter what.

In the good times—anniversaries, birthdays, or other celebrations—take the opportunity to reaffirm your love and dedication to one another. These moments are important, as they allow you to express gratitude for the relationship and to recognize how far you've come together. These happy occasions are natural reminders to cherish each other and celebrate the bond you've built. But they're not the only times when reaffirming your commitment matters.

It's just as crucial to demonstrate your dedication when things are tough. Whether you're facing financial struggles, personal challenges, or conflicts within the relationship, letting your partner know that you're still fully committed can make a huge difference. During these moments, a simple gesture—like expressing, "I'm still here, and I'm not going anywhere"—can offer a sense of security that words alone can't fully capture. It shows your partner that your love and commitment aren't conditional; they're unwavering, even when life throws unexpected difficulties your way.

In difficult times, reaffirming your commitment strengthens your bond. It reassures your partner that, despite the current struggles, you're still in this together, working side by side. This mutual reassurance builds resilience in the relationship, reminding both of you that tough times are temporary, but the commitment you've made to each other is lasting. Knowing you can rely on each other, no matter what life brings, creates a foundation of trust that can withstand any storm.

It's not just about verbal affirmations either—showing your commitment through action is just as important, if not more. Don't wait for a major event to tell your partner how much they mean to you. Make a habit of regularly expressing your love and commitment, whether it's through a heartfelt conversation, small acts of kindness, or simply being present when they need you. Sometimes, just showing up and being there for your partner during a rough patch speaks louder than words. Your consistent presence and support remind them that they're not alone and that your commitment goes beyond just words.

Special occasions can be wonderful opportunities to celebrate your relationship and reaffirm your commitment, but the ordinary, everyday moments count just as much. In the quiet times, when there's no celebration to mark, you can still show your dedication by being fully present, offering a kind word, or doing something thoughtful that reinforces your love. And when difficulties arise, take the time to have open, honest conversations about your commitment. Reassure your partner that, despite the challenges, your dedication to them remains steady. These conversations can provide immense comfort, especially when things feel uncertain.

One way to consistently demonstrate your commitment is by establishing rituals that help reaffirm your bond. These rituals don't have to be elaborate—a weekly date night, a quiet coffee together in the morning, or a monthly check-in conversation can do wonders for maintaining a sense of connection. These intentional moments remind both of you that the relationship is a priority, and that your commitment to each other is being nurtured regularly.

It's also important to actively support each other's personal goals and dreams. Commitment isn't just about staying together—it's about helping each other grow, both individually and as a couple. Show your dedication by being your partner's biggest supporter, whether that means encouraging them to pursue a new passion or being there for them during moments of self-doubt. When your partner sees that you're not only committed to the relationship but to their personal growth, it strengthens the trust and bond between you.

When challenges arise, face them together as a team. Approach conflicts or tough times with the mindset that you're both on the same side. Discuss your commitment openly and make a plan to work through the issues together. This united front reinforces the idea that no matter what comes your way, you'll handle it together. Your partner will feel reassured knowing that they have someone by their side who's committed to weathering life's ups and downs, no matter how difficult they may be.

In the end, demonstrating commitment in marriage is about consistently showing up for each other, in both the joyful moments and the difficult ones. It's about making sure your partner knows they're loved, supported, and valued, no matter what's happening in life. By clarifying and affirming your commitment in both good times and bad, you reinforce the strength of your relationship, building a bond that can endure anything. It's the daily, intentional acts of love and support that keep your marriage strong and thriving, ensuring that both of you feel secure in the knowledge that your commitment is unshakable.

COMMITMENT VS. COMPATIBILITY

In a marriage, commitment is the bedrock that keeps everything else intact. While compatibility and emotions certainly play a role, they tend to fluctuate—sometimes more often than we realize. Emotions can be unpredictable, and compatibility might not always align perfectly as life shifts. This is why commitment must take priority over everything else. A strong commitment ensures that even when your feelings change or when you and your partner don't see eye to eye, you remain dedicated to working through the challenges and growing together. It's that steadfast dedication that keeps a relationship thriving through all of life's ups and downs.

Compatibility, while important, should come second to commitment. There will be times when you and your partner don't share the same interests, perspectives, or approaches to things. Maybe your hobbies have changed over time, or perhaps you handle stress in completely different ways. These differences don't have to be deal-breakers. In fact, they're often what makes a relationship dynamic and interesting. What matters more than being perfectly compatible is your commitment to each other. It's the glue that holds you together when those differences feel more pronounced. And when emotions fluctuate—when one of you is up and the other is down—it's your shared commitment that keeps you grounded, reminding you that you're in this together, no matter what.

Commitment is what creates long-term stability in your relationship. It's the steady force that remains constant, even when life feels uncertain. Life will inevitably bring challenges—financial struggles, health issues, external pressures—but when your commitment to each other is strong, you're better equipped to navigate those tough times together. Unlike emotions, which can change from moment to moment, commitment offers a sense of security. It's knowing that no matter how difficult things get, you're both dedicated to weathering the storm together. This foundation of stability allows your relationship to endure beyond the fleeting feelings of the moment, offering something solid to lean on during life's unpredictability.

A strong commitment also builds deep trust. When you know that your partner is fully committed to you—through thick and thin—it creates a sense of security that allows both of you to be vulnerable, open, and honest. You're not left wondering if a rough patch will be the end of the relationship because you trust that your partner is as dedicated to working through it as you are. This kind of trust is essential for the long-term health of your marriage, and it only comes when commitment takes precedence over everything else.

Commitment is ultimately a choice, and it's a choice you have to make consciously. It's about deciding that your relationship, and the person you're building that relationship with, is worth the effort. It's not about perfection or waiting for everything to line up just right. Instead, it's about making the decision every day to prioritize your marriage above any temporary incompatibilities or emotional highs and lows. Regularly remind each other of that commitment—don't let it go unspoken. Talk about it openly and express your dedication to making the relationship work, no matter what obstacles arise.

It's also essential to demonstrate your commitment through action. Words are important, but actions speak louder. Show your partner that you're committed by being present, by supporting them when they need it most, and by working together to overcome challenges. Whether it's through the daily little things, like offering encouragement or helping out when they're feeling overwhelmed, or through bigger actions, like facing difficult decisions together, these demonstrations of commitment strengthen the bond between you.

There are several practical steps you can take to keep commitment at the forefront of your relationship. First, make sure you're putting in consistent effort. Relationships require ongoing attention, and that means being intentional about nurturing your connection. Daily acts of kindness, regular check-ins, or simply making time to spend together are all ways to ensure that your commitment remains a priority.

Handling conflicts with care is another crucial aspect. When disagreements arise, remember that you're on the same team. Approach the conflict with a commitment mindset, focusing on resolving the issue in a way that strengthens the relationship, not weakens it. When you approach challenges with the understanding that your relationship is worth fighting for, it becomes easier to navigate those difficult moments together.

Celebrating milestones, like anniversaries or significant moments in your journey, is also a great way to reaffirm your commitment. These occasions provide an opportunity to reflect on how far you've come and to celebrate the fact that, through it all, you've chosen each other. Use these celebrations to remind yourselves of the commitment you've made and to look forward to the future you're building together.

At the heart of it all, commitment is about choosing each other every day. It's about making the decision to stay dedicated, even when things are tough, even when compatibility isn't perfect, and even when emotions are running high. When commitment is the cornerstone of your marriage, it ensures that the relationship is built on a solid foundation—one that can withstand the inevitable ups and downs of life. This kind of unwavering commitment is what creates a lasting and fulfilling marriage, allowing you to grow together and face whatever comes your way with confidence and unity.

CLOSING SUMMARY

Commitment in a relationship goes beyond promises or vows—it's about making a conscious choice every single day to prioritize and nurture your partnership. In Chapter 12: Commitment, we explored how true commitment isn't just about the good times, but especially about standing by each other during life's challenges. It's those daily decisions to show up, support one another, and invest in your relationship that keep the love alive and strong, even when things get tough.

We got into what commitment really means, emphasizing that it's a continuous effort rather than a one-time declaration. Understanding and communicating your commitment regularly helps build a foundation of trust and security. Whether it's through small gestures, open conversations, or supporting each other's personal growth, demonstrating your dedication reinforces the bond you share. Commitment isn't about perfection; it's about consistently choosing each other and working together to overcome any obstacles that come your way.

Ultimately, commitment is the bedrock of a lasting and fulfilling marriage. It ensures that your relationship remains resilient and adaptable, no matter how much you and your partner grow and change over time. By prioritizing commitment, you create a partnership built on trust, mutual respect, and unwavering support. This steadfast dedication transforms your relationship into a true union of hearts and minds, capable of weathering any storm and celebrating every joy together. Remember, it's those everyday choices to love and support each other that make your marriage not just survive, but truly thrive.

Marriage Tip

Try affirming your commitment to one another during or after your next fight. Tell your partner that at the end of the day, you believe in what you both have and that you're on the same team.

CONCLUSION

As we turn the final page of *Forever and Ever*, I hope you feel a renewed sense of hope and empowerment for your marriage. This journey through the chapters has been about understanding, growth, and the enduring power of love. Together, we've explored how each of you loves and communicates differently, navigates emotions, and builds a life filled with intimacy and trust.

One of the most profound lessons I've learned through countless marriage counseling sessions is the simple yet transformative question I always begin with: "Do you want to be together?" This question cuts to the heart of what truly matters. When both partners answer "yes," it creates a foundation of mutual commitment that makes overcoming any challenge possible. It's not just about wanting to stay together; it's about choosing each other every single day, no matter what life throws your way.

Throughout this book, we've gone over the depths of how you and your partner express love, handle conflicts, set expectations, and adapt to life's inevitable changes. We've looked at practical strategies for managing finances, parenting, and time, all while maintaining the spark that keeps your relationship vibrant. We've also emphasized the importance of emotional transparency, forgiveness, and unwavering commitment.

But beyond all the strategies and insights, the heart of *Forever and Ever* is about the enduring desire to remain united. When both of you genuinely want to be together, you unlock a limitless potential to grow, adapt, and thrive as a couple. This shared intention transforms obstacles into opportunities for deeper connection and understanding.

As you close this book, remember that marriage is not a static destination but a dynamic, ongoing journey. It requires continuous effort, patience, and above all, a steadfast commitment to each other. Embrace the lessons you've learned here, and let them guide you in building a relationship that is resilient, loving, and fulfilling.

Believe in the power of your commitment. Trust in your ability to communicate openly and adapt together. Cherish the intimacy and trust you cultivate, and never lose sight of your shared desire to be together. When both partners hold this intention close, they open the door to endless possibilities and a future filled with love and happiness.

May your marriage be a testament to love's enduring strength—a partnership where both of you flourish, supporting and uplifting each other every step of the way. Remember, when you both say "yes" to each other, truly, anything is possible.

Thank you for allowing me to be a part of your journey. Here's to a lifetime of love, joy, and togetherness.

With great expectations,

STAY CONNECTED

Thank you for joining me on this journey through *Forever and Ever*. I'm truly honored to be a part of your path toward a stronger, more fulfilling marriage. Let's continue this conversation and support each other beyond the pages of this book. Here are several ways you can stay connected with me and access more resources to enrich your relationship:

Website

www.homerhargrove.com

Social Media

Facebook: *@homerdh3* | Instagram: *@homerdh3* | LinkedIn: *@homerdh3*

Books

- *Feed My Sheep: 90 Day Devotion for Spiritual Growth*
- *Feed My Lambs: A 6-Month Christian Kids' Curriculum For Ages 5 10*

Podcast

- *Hidden Potential: A Guide For Ministry Leadership*

Workshops

Participate in interactive workshops based on the principles of *Forever and Ever*. These sessions offer hands-on guidance, practical strategies, and the opportunity to connect with other couples.

Speaking Engagements

If you are looking to spark a fire in your audience, invite me as a speaker to your event! Let me set the momentum and tone for growth through one of my talks. Talks are available in person or virtual.

Online Store

Check out my online store to see if there a fresh design that's right for you! With each design that I make, my hope is that it would not only look fire but help encourage others like it did for me.

Connect Personally

I value each connection and am here to support you on your journey. Feel free to reach out with your stories, questions, or feedback. Let's continue to grow together in love and understanding.

Thank You

Thank you for allowing me to be a part of your story. Together, we can create marriages that are not only lasting but also deeply joyful and fulfilling. I look forward to staying connected and supporting you every step of the way.

Made in the USA
Columbia, SC
03 October 2024